Thomas Bernhard:
Essential Companions
and Legacy

edited by

Martin Huber
Manfred Mittermayer
Peter Karlhuber

Imprint

Publishers:	Land Oberösterreich,
	Adalbert-Stifter-Institut des Landes Oberösterreich
	Adalbert-Stifter-Platz 1, A-4020 Linz
	Director: Johann Lachinger
Editors:	Martin Huber, Manfred Mittermayer, Peter Karlhuber
Translation:	Jan Bullen, Douglas Gill, Christina Guenther
Layout:	Gerhard Spring, Peter Karlhuber
Colour reproduction:	Petra Egg
Printing:	Agens-Werk Geyer + Reisser, Vienna

© 2001: Adalbert-Stifter-Institut, Thomas Bernhard Nachlaßverwaltung GmbH., the authors – otherwise see acknowledgments

This book is published as a special edition in the series ›Literatur im StifterHaus‹ on the occasion of the exhibition ›Thomas Bernhard: Essential Companions and Legacy‹ (Vienna, Linz 2001)

Conception:	Martin Huber, Manfred Mittermayer
Design concept:	Peter Karlhuber
Project management:	Petra-Maria Dallinger, Regina Pintar
Produced by:	Adalbert-Stifter-Institut des Landes Oberösterreich
	Institut für Kulturförderung des Landes Oberösterreich,
	Thomas-Bernhard-Privatstiftung,
	Österreichische Nationalbibliothek
Exhibition construction:	Hannes Stockinger, Klaus Hammerschmidt
Decoration:	Edgar Fontanari, Fa. Gorth, Fa. Wawrein, Ernst Wolzenburg
Photo development:	Foto Leutner, Vienna
Film and audio research:	Helga Reimair, Peter Karlhuber, Martin Huber
Film and audio editing:	Gerhard Spring

The team would like to thank the following for their support:

James Abram (Großgmain), Margit Auli (StifterHaus Linz), Marie-Christine Baratta-Dragono (Thomas Bernhard Privatstiftung, Vienna), Rudolf Brändle (Vienna/Salzburg), Elisabeth Brandstötter (Bundesministerium für Bildung, Wissenschaft und Kultur), Ingrid Bülau (Hamburg), Edith Czap (Burghauptmannschaft, Vienna), Jörg Dasch (SFB), Anne Marie Fabjan (Gmunden), Raimund Fellinger (Suhrkamp Verlag Frankfurt am Main), Manuela Friedrich (HR), Christina Guenther (Salzburg/Bowling Green, USA), Petra Christina Hardt (Suhrkamp Verlag Frankfurt am Main), Hildemar Holl (Universität Salzburg), Hans Höller (Universität Salzburg), Chris Ives (Oberndorf), Peter Kautzky (ORF), Brigitte Keusch (HR), Anton Knoll (Österreichische Nationalbibliothek, Vienna), André Krüger (WDR), Alexandra Kuhn (Vienna), Gerda Maleta (Vienna/Oberweis), Gwendolyne Melchinger (Vienna), Rudolf Neuböck (Pinsdorf), Marion Oberdorfer (ORF), Kurt Osinger (Vienna), Richard Pils (Bibliothek der Provinz Weitra), Gisela Prossnitz (Salzburger Festspiele), Ferry Radax (Vienna/Hollenburg), Bernhard Sandbichler (Residenz Verlag Salzburg), Wendelin Schmidt-Dengler (Österreichisches Literaturarchiv), Gerhard Schuster (Vienna), Paul Stepanek (Institut für Kulturförderung Linz), Christian Strasser (Henndorf), Liselotte von Uexküll (Vienna), Siegfried Unseld (Suhrkamp Verlag Frankfurt am Main), Christina Voigt (Deutsches Rundfunkarchiv), Astrid Wallner (Literaturhaus, Vienna), Gerlinde von Wittich (SFB).

The research on Thomas Bernhard´s unpublished works has been made possible by a grant from the Austrian Ministery of Education, Science and Culture.

ISBN: 3-900424-27-6

Contents

Preface

In a short prose text that appeared in 1978 in *Der Stimmenimitator/The Voice Impersonator*, Thomas Bernhard describes how a tribute to an author can turn into the opposite if one becomes too familiar with the artist: ›The closer we get to an author after the inital encounter, the greater we in fact distance ourselves from him; the deeper we delve into the personality of the author, the greater we distance ourselves from his work. Every word that he utters, each thought that he articulates in our presence separates us further from his oeuvre.‹

Nonetheless, the exhibition ›Thomas Bernhard: Essential Companions and Legacy‹, which will be mounted in Vienna and Linz during 2001 following the 70th birthday of the author, attempts to come to closer terms with the complex personality of the artist. It links Bernhard's life with his work by connecting the writings that Bernhard inherited from key figures in his life with his own literary remains, texts that will be presented here to the public for the first time. This approach will not only provide insight into facts, personal references and background material but also into the history of the origin of Bernhard's texts and the peculiarities of his writing.

Since 1999 Martin Huber has been working at the Thomas-Bernhard-Archive in Gmunden towards making accessible in a systematic way Bernhard's literary remains. Throughout the year 2001 the prestigious Villa Stonborough-Wittgenstein is being adapted to house this archive permanently. The Province of Upper Austria is providing financial support for this endeavour. Bernhard's estate will be made available to researchers there. For this reason, it is timely to publish a sort of a prefatory report on the preliminary assessment of the estate.

Selected texts from Bernhard's literary works constitute the central part of the exhibition (and of the book). We not only document in chronological order the various versions of a given text but also offer a juxtaposition of different developmental stages of specific texts. The distinct modes in which Bernhard edited his texts are quite literally rendered ›readable‹. The different phases of writing demonstrate Thomas Bernhard's continuous process of self-excavation that began early in his life and only ended with his death. His published works represent only stages in a far more complex series of trajectories. A second important section of the exhibition contains numerous photographs from all areas of his life which were never shown to the public in this way. It constitutes a pictoral biography taken from the private possession of the author, a private addendum, so to speak, to the better known professional photographs.

The estates of Bernhard´s grandfather Johannes Freumbichler and of his ›life companion‹ Hedwig Stavianicek, the most important people in his life, also are presented within the context of Bernhard's estate. They represent very different collections of documents: On the one hand, there are the life testaments and numerous unpublished manuscripts of Freumbichler, the primarily unsuccessful writer from the province of Salzburg, who served as model for all the failed artist figures in Bernhard's works. On the other hand, there are the letters and writings of the life-long companion and confidante which offer insight into the nature of the unusual relationship between Stavianicek and the significantly younger artist.

Freumbichler's and Stavianicek's estates were already the object of smaller exhibitions. On the occasion of the 10th anniversary of Bernhard's death on 12 February 1999 (which coincided almost exactly with the 50th anniversary of Freumbichler's death on 11 February of the same year) Manfred Mittermayer designed the exhibition ›Johannes Freumbichler – Thomas Bernhard‹ at Bernhard's Ohlsdorf residence. As early as 1996 Bernhard's sister Susanne Kuhn organized an exhibition at the same location documenting Hedwig Stavianicek's life.

For the first time, significant aspects of the earlier exhibitions are now being combined with those segments of Bernhard's estate which inform us about his work as an author. The fact that these two most important people in Bernhard's life had a crucial impact on his writing is made evident in the way in which this volume is organized: The interplay between the biographical data and Bernhard's work is highlighted as often as possible. The significance of the grandfather as point of departure for this literature thereby becomes clear even if the grandson early in life took leave from Freumbichler's aesthetic concept and moved ›in the opposite direction‹ (*The Cellar*). The importance of his life-long partner as driving force and anchor who provided access to new societal spheres of experience also becomes evident.

Martin Huber developed that section in the exhibition and the catalogue that focuses on Bernhard's literary remains. Manfred Mittermayer is the author of the sections on Freumbichler and Stavianicek. As in the case of the earlier Johannes Freumbichler Exhibition in Ohlsdorf, Peter Karlhuber carried out the artistic realization of this entire ›encounter‹ with Thomas Bernhard and his ›essential companions‹.

Such a project would of course not have been possible without the friendship and support of Bernhard's siblings, Peter Fabjan and Susanne Kuhn. The editors of this catalogue and the organizers of the exhibition are very thankful to both.

Our heartfelt thanks also to Petra-Maria Dallinger of the Institut für Kulturförderung of the Province of Upper Austria and to Regina Pintar of the Adalbert-Stifter-Institut in Linz for the idea for this project and for their efficient assistance.

The Editors

Johannes Freumbichler

1881-1949

[...] any young person, if possible, goes as often as he can to see the one person he knows and loves best – in my case, my grandfather.

An Indication of the Cause

If it hadn't been for his grandfather
our friend would still have his naturalness today

The Soprano regarding the Bass in *The Celebrities*

Johannes Freumbichler,
Traunstein 1943

Thomas Bernhard with
his grandfather on occa-
sion of his confirmation,
Traunstein 1943

10

›My maternal grandfather‹.

Johannes Freumbichler in Bernhard's Literature

Manfred Mittermayer

1.

In Thomas Bernhard's prose as well as in his dramas, especially towards the end of his literary career, one repeatedly comes across sentences that can be read as aphorisms about man and his existence. It is a collection of statements in the generalising ›we‹-form in which fundamental observations of his main characters are laid down – a store of philosophical perceptions which of course are not infrequently reproduced in ironic modification.

One of these passages is in the autobiographical volume *Ein Kind/A Child* (1982), and in it the image of his maternal grandfather takes shape more clearly than anywhere else, an image that has already been sketched in many memorable scenes in the previous four books, *Die Ursache/An Indication of the Cause* (1975), *Der Keller/The Cellar* (1976), *Der Atem/Breath* (1978) and *Die Kälte/In the Cold* (1981):

Grandfathers are our teachers, our real philosophers. They are the people who pull open the curtain that others are always closing. When we are with them, we see things as they really are – not just the auditorium but the stage and all that goes on behind the scenes. For thousands of years grandfathers have taken it upon themselves to create the devil where otherwise there would only have been God. Through them we see the drama in all its fullness, not just a pathetic, bowdlerized fragment, for what it is: pure farce.

(GE 10)

It is here that Bernhard combines a succession of decisive elements from his literary world at whose centre he places the ›philosopher‹, who provides man with an understanding of his existence. In so doing he uses a metaphor which runs through his work from the beginning: All in all the world is just a theatre, life within society takes place as if on a stage on which everything is seen in a euphemistic version of what is much less satisfying in reality. It is therefore all the more important to see through the outward forms of reality, to unmask the world's play and its actors. This is precisely what Thomas Bernhard's literature is devoted to, in a particular way.

What is quoted here comes, to a certain extent, at the end of the author's autobiographical self-seeking. Over one and a half years previously, this theme appears for the first time in Bernhard's prose. In the year 1968 Bernhard published the essay *Unsterblichkeit ist unmöglich*/*Immortality is Impossible*, in which, for the first time, he himself gave information about his early life in literary form. In this text the grandson's relationship to his grandfather, Johannes Freumbichler, is described as an ideally structured partnership in the shelter of which, life, exposed to extreme danger in war and in times of need, can be saved by means of science and philosophy:

I discovered, I probably could not speak yet, a philosopher, who had discovered me: my grandfather. We play a game that lasts twelve years, until his death, and in which I (because I am the grandson) have never lost: I am introduced to the sciences and the arts.

(TLB 28)

In his autobiography Bernhard also continues with the description of the teacher who impressed his grandson in such a fundamental way during his early childhood and youth. His pleasantest memories were those of the walks with his grandfather, as he emphasizes in *An Indication of the Cause*: ›We used to walk for hours in the country, and I would listen to his observations, by means of which he gradually taught me the art of observation. I was attentive to everything be pointed out to me.‹ He positively refers to the time with Freumbichler as the ›only useful education I had, for it had a decisive effect on my whole life‹, adding, ›It was he and no other who taught me everything about life, who acquainted me with life by first acquainting me with nature. Everything

I know I owe to this man, who decisively influenced my whole life and my whole existence‹ (GE 129).

Especially as far as his function as teacher is concerned, however, Freumbichler's image in the autobiography is not only a positive one. One certainly cannot claim that Bernhard exclusively glorified his grandfather; for all the fond descriptions, the other sides of this contradictory personality are not suppressed at all. Thus the narrator in *An Indication of the Cause*, in his account of what he had to endure day after day whilst attending grammar school in Salzburg, openly blames his grandfather and what he had taught him for his taking the wrong path.

My grandfather of all people ought to have known that he himself had disqualified me for this kind of school as a preparation for life by the training he had given me. How could I have suddenly fitted in at a school like this when in fact I had been carefully and painstakingly educated by him all my life to reject all *conventional* education. He was *the only teacher I acknowledged*, and in many respects this is still so.

(GE 132)

Thus the fact that his grandfather had sent him to a grammar school, and in so doing exposed him ›to the rigours of life in Salzburg‹, was to the grandson ›bound to seem like a betrayal‹ (ibid.). With the distance of an adult remembering the past the author keenly analyses what lay behind his grandfather's educational aims: ›His object was without doubt to secure for his grandson what he himself had never had: a *proper education* in Salzburg, which was his home town and mine‹ (GE 130). ›I think of you every day and hope that you are studying *hard* and that your final marks are *at least* average. Think every day of your high aim: University!‹, are the words Freumbichler actually uses in a letter from that time which Bernhard kept, together with photographs and other personal objects that were important to him, in a glass cupboard in his house in Ohlsdorf.

Thus the path ›*in the opposite direction*‹, chanted repeatedly in the first pages of *The Cellar* (this expression is used more than twenty times here), is also a step away from his grandfather's influence – at least from the problematic side of this relationship. According to the author it was the moment he dropped out of school which was ›the one moment which was decisive for my later life‹ (GE 174), and he describes it as a step towards existential self-seeking – ›Now I'm going to myself, and every day I get closer and closer to myself‹, he thought, and finally ›that I was *now on the right route*‹ (GE 152). ›I found *the other people* by going *in the opposite direction*, no longer to the odious grammar school but to the apprenticeship which was the saving of me‹, is the first sentence of the book (GE 145). ›My grandfather, on whom I had pinned *all* my hopes, had himself come to the end of the road and could no longer point me the way ahead‹, Bernhard writes in a later paragraph. ›What I had learnt from him was suddenly of use only as far as my imagination was concerned and had no bearing upon my practical life. And so all at once I felt myself deserted by the one person I had trusted one hundred percent‹ (GE 171f.).

2.

What is particularly noticeable in Bernhard's autobiography is the extent to which he expressly associates his grandfather's influence with language. ›He was my great explainer, the first, the most important, basically the only one‹, Bernhard writes in the concluding volume *A Child*.

He would point to animals and plants with his stick and deliver a short lecture on every plant to which his stick drew my attention. It is important to know what one is looking at. Gradually one

Johannes Freumbichler, Seekirchen around 1936

must learn at least to put a name to everything. One must know where it comes from, what it is.

(GE 35)

Even the earliest word that the narrator of the autobiography attributes to himself is ›grandfather‹ (GE 27). He is addressing the most important person of his early years with whom he could discuss everything, the one to whom he owes the medium (of language) with which he was to make a name for himself later as a writer (with far more success than the one addressed here).

In Bernhard's autobiography his literary career is clearly presented as succeeding that of his grandfather's. When, on his death, he gives up the position of writer previously held by him in an exemplary way, the grandson takes his place. ›My grandfather had been a writer, and he was now dead‹, wrote Bernhard in *In the Cold*. ›Now I was entitled to write; now myself had the chance‹ (GE 291). There is even written proof of this *translatio* of authorship. As from one king to the next the insignia (of writing) are passed on when the narrator in *Breath* talks of the grandfather's estate in his last will and testament:

Among the objects he bequeathed to me was his typewriter, bought at an auction in the Dorotheum in Vienna in the early 1920s, on which he made what he called the fair copies of all his works. I still use this typewriter, an American L.C. Smith, which is probably over sixty years old, for typing my own works.

(GE 257)

13

Johannes Freumbichler,
Traunstein 1939

The grandfather's function as guarantor for his grandson's vindicating self-assertion through the medium of language is reproduced in a positively model way at the beginning of *A Child*. A secret bicycle ride, which at first gives the young boy the feeling of being ›master of the world‹, ends with a mighty crash which he experiences at the same time as being ›suddenly reverted headlong into childhood‹ (GE 7). In order to be able to stand the dreaded encounter with his mother he chooses a genuinely literary strategy. When he explains how the accident happened he turns the events around to mean the contrary: ›At the end of it I was able, by a few short sentences, to turn my pathetic failure into triumph‹ (GE 16). With the help of this account, which he calls ›a very successful work of art‹ (ibid.), he really does manage to avoid being punished by his mother. After a successful ›main rehearsal‹ at his friend Schorschi's, he performs the ›work of art‹ for his grandfather whom he is able to win over as his partner in league against his mother. For the first time it is language which saves the author-to-be in extreme danger. This is assuming that the grandfather authorizes it, ›the authority to whom everyone deferred, who sorted out every disagreement and whose word was law. He was the judge, the one who passed sentence.‹ (GE 8)

In his grandson's literary work of art the grandfather, in a quite specific way, becomes

the bearer of those words which he himself placed in his pupil. For, analogous to the form of communication on the endless walks during which the grandson mostly ›was strictly forbidden to speak‹ (GE 35), there later developed one of the characteristics of Bernhard's texts, their unusual narrative structure. Just as the grandson had once been the receiving instrument for his grandfather's monologues, in most of his prose a largely undefined narrator is exposed to the monologues of an authority on language whose words constitute his own speech (and therefore also the literary text). To what extent the overpowering flow of language of a protagonist dominates the dialogue in Bernhard's dramas (so far as there is one), is demonstrated repeatedly in each of the author's 18 plays. One could literally say: The text constantly re-produces the way its author received language in his early life. At the same time, however, the increasing attempt of the first-person narrator to gradually detach himself from his fateful surrender to the dominant main characters (a comparison of the novels *Frost* and *Correction* makes this development quite clear) demonstrates the continuous search for independence that is given shape in this literature.

3.

By which means we arrive at the very aspect of the relationship between Bernhard and his grandfather which presents itself in the most complicated way, whose analysis, however, particularly illuminates the literary process used by the author. In his TV monologue *Drei Tage/Three Days* (1971), Bernhard himself affirmed the basic conformity of his fictional characters with Freumbichler in a much quoted statement: ›[..] that is all in the books later, and these characters, male characters, that's always my maternal grandfather‹ (TBL 10). Of course such an unequivocal declaration does not justify either the assumption that Freumbichler and Bernhard's protagonists are really one and the same person. In any case the point in question is the complex transfer of real material into a fictional, artificial world. But at the same time it cannot be denied how many analogies can be established between biographical data or the grandfather's written accounts and the corresponding passages in his grandson's texts.

Thus the comparison between the ›real‹ person, Johannes Freumbichler, and his literary variation can give an impression of how Bernhard's artistic method works: how the author gathers his poetic vocabulary in the reality of his own experience, how he uses the models formed from this throughout his literature – and how he then enriches them in a decisive way with added layers of meaning. For this purpose we are going to consider a series of five plays in chronological order in which reference is made to the figure of the grandfather in various nuances. The earliest of these plays was published just before the author began his autobiographical self-investigation, the last appeared exactly ten years later, shortly after the publication of *A Child*. At the same time a further characteristic of Bernhard's literary development is discernible: the increasing irony in the material that he continues to imagine and re-imagine, and with it also the ever more masterful way he dealt with the themes and contents of his art.

The film director, Ferry Radax, who created Bernhard's most informative self-representation in the above mentioned monologue (*Three Days*), emphasizes, in an interview, that the affinity Bernhard is known to have felt with the actor, Bernhard Minetti, is attributable to the similarity of appearance between him and his grandfather. Minetti had already performed his first part in a Bernhard play: the General, in the Berlin production of *Die Jagdgesellschaft/ The Hunting Party* (1974). He became *the* Bernhard actor, however, in the Salzburg Festival production of the comedy *Die Macht der Gewohnheit/The Force of Habit* (in the

same year – 1974). The play centres on the vain attempts of a circus manager to put on a performance of Schubert's quintet *The Trout* with his co-performers in the circus ring. All the human striving for perfection finally proves to be in vain – a typical Bernhard theme, therefore. Moreover, it is a play about power, about the subjection of people in the name of art. With the example of Caribaldi who drives his four fellow actors into hell every day during the rehearsals for Schubert's quintet, Bernhard demonstrates what it means when a person gives in completely to an idea (in this case an artistic one) and in so doing invests not only his own existence in it but also that of the people around him:

In art
especially in feats of art
there is no mercy [...]
the only possibility
is ruthlessness

(St I/316, 319)

Here, Caribaldi uses actually one of the keywords typical of many of Bernhard's characters – the demand for ›ruthlessness‹ appears particularly often, for example in the author's first play for the Salzburg Festival: *Der Ignorant und der Wahnsinnige/The Ignoramus and the Madman* (1972). In Freumbichler's notebooks, those records he kept for years, in which he wrote down a kind of intellectual soliloquy, the term appears time and again. ›To be able to live completely for myself, totally in my way, I go to extremes, if necessary even to the point of ruthlessness and cruelty‹, he notes in about 1943. ›He had incarcerated himself with his writing, with his literary task, yet he allowed himself the freedom of being alone and subordinating everything else to his life's work‹, Bernhard put it in his autobiographical volume *The Cellar*. ›All his life he made those around him suffer, above all his wife, my grandmother, but also my mother, it was their tireless devotion that made it possible for him to live in this state of total creative isolation.‹ (GE 184)

Johannes Freumbichler,
Traunstein 1939

everyone and everything‹, is how Minetti describes the situation before starting his vain attempt to make a stage comeback once more. The key-word regarding his attitude to the audience is ›against‹, and he repeats it with the obstinacy peculiar to him:

against the audience
against
against
against
again and again against

(St II/216)

The madness
of a single person
which this person ruthlessly
drives all others into

(St I/294)

is how the animal tamer in *The Force of Habit* comments on the power-structure which he himself belongs to in the role of a victim. ›I have to go mad – or I am lost. I don't care about anything else and think only of my projects day and night‹, writes Johannes Freumbichler in one of his notebooks from the year 1912. ›It must be easy for me to sacrifice everything for my work!!!!‹ he notes one year later. ›What I strive for must happen or life will be worth nothing at all to me. To achieve this I need your complete and unconditional help‹, is what Freumbichler writes in one of his letters to Anna Bernhard, his life companion, from the year 1926. At that point he was living more or less exclusively on the proceeds of her work or on the donations from his daughter, Herta.

In 1976, Bernhard paid special tribute to his favourite actor in his play *Minetti*, whose main character is an actor of the same name. This character clearly bears features of Bernhard's grandfather – especially his sorrowful isolation in an environment basically perceived as hostile: ›Finished with people / finished with

›My aversion to people borders on madness‹, writes Freumbichler in one of his notebooks (ca. 1942). ›In their deepest wretchedness people feel only bitter envy, even hate for the beautiful, good and unique things that a man has made!! That is the truth.‹ Just like the characters in his grandson's plays he retreats in bitterness to the last refuge left to him: ›Extreme egotism is the only right rule of life for exceptional people. Everything else is deception‹, he notes one year later. At this point one is struck by the quite particular variation of the literary game he is carrying on with his grandfather's estate: Here, as in various other passages from Freumbichler's notebooks, one finds the structural elements with which the grandson's characters just as frequently endeavour to give force to what they have to say – as randomly chosen examples: ›We only go to cemeteries‹, says Oehler in *Gehen/Walking* (1971), ›to bury a genius who was ruined by the state and driven to his death, that is the truth‹ (G 37), and the writer in *The Hunting Party* postulates: ›A person / is a desperate person / everything else is a lie‹ (St I/221). Thus Freumbichler's voice is even echoed in the idiom of Bernhard's literary characters.

The image of the grandfather as a philosopher, which one encounters quite early on in connection with Freumbichler, is taken up again in one of Bernhard's most successful plays, written during the phase of his autobiographical project. The main character in the comedy *Der Weltverbesserer/The Reformer of the World* (1979) is a private scholar whose treatise on improving the world, which has recently been awarded a distinction by the university, basically lays down only one main thought: ›The world is a cesspit / which stinks / this cesspit needs clearing out‹. He adds, of course, ›there is nothing else left for us to do / but plunge headlong into‹ (St III/166). It is remarkable that this same statement is not attributed to the grandfather until later, in the autobiographical text *In the Cold*, which was published in 1981. Bernhard followed this line of practice on several occasions, as we shall see: Before according Freumbichler himself with the real details, he first tried them out in fictional, experimental form. Then, however, he actually wrote:

My grandfather had been right in his judgement of the world: it was indeed a cesspit, but one which engendered the most intricate and beautiful forms if one looked into it long enough, if one's eye was prepared for such strenuous and microscopic observation. It was a cesspit which yielded up its own natural beauties to the sharp revolutionary gaze. Yet whoever contemplates it for long, whoever spends decades gazing into it, eventually becomes exhausted and dies, or plunges headlong into it.

(GE 305)

But the ›reformer of the world‹ also expresses fundamental doubts as to the ability of philosophy to come to terms with life in such a way as it still appeared from the perspective of the essay *Immortality is Impossible*:

I once trusted Montaigne
too much
then Pascal
too much
then Voltaire
then Schopenhauer
We keep hanging on these philosophical wall
hooks

until they become loose
and if we tug on them all our life
we pull everything down

(St III/177)

Shortly after this, Bernhard's character, Wertheimer in *Der Untergeher/The Loser* (1983), breaks in a much more radical way with the philosophical patterns for explaining the world: ›If we look at things squarely the only thing left from the greatest philosophical enterprises is a pitiful aphoristic aftertaste, he said, no matter what the philosophy, no matter what the philosopher, everything falls to bits‹ (Lo 65). And he expands his findings to include every idea of ›greatness‹ when he adds: ›In the end the so-called great minds wind up in a state where we can only feel pity for their ridiculousness, their pitifulness‹ (Lo 66). Once again, a similar statement in connection with his grandfather was made only shortly before in one of Bernhard's autobiographical volumes (*A Child*): ›Always have something great in view: that

Johannes Freumbichler, Ettendorf near Traunstein (where he lived from 1938 to 1946)

17

was his constant exhortation. Fix your eyes on what is highest! Always on what is highest! But what was the highest? When we look around, we find ourselves surrounded only by the ludicrous and the pathetic‹ (GE 36).

In 1981, the same year in which *In the Cold* appeared, the play *Am Ziel/Arrived*, was performed at the Salzburg Festival. It is a text which, perhaps more than others, can be interpreted on one of its levels of meaning as a game the author plays with the elements of his own biography. After a triumphant stage success, a dramatist is received at a house situated on the Dutch coast. It belongs to an old lady who is called ›The mother‹ in the dramatis personae. Both are the creations of an author whose problematic relationship with his own mother had its beginnings, as we know, in the same geographical area – as he relates, one year later, in the autobiographical volume *A Child*. And the ›mother‹ assures her guest, whom she more or less ›adopts‹: ›You have made something of yourself / you can read about it in all the papers [...] You have nothing to fear‹ (St III/362). ›You have arrived Sir‹ (St III/379). Also in *A Child* Bernhard passes on the very sentences with which his own mother virtually denied his existence: ›*You're a nothing* [..]! *You're worthless*‹, is what Bernhard was told as a child (GE 16). In his literary fiction (and through its success) he therefore refutes the judgement passed on him in his early life from the mother's position of power.

Bernhard seldom refers in such an overtly ironic way to the experiences and traumas in his life as he does in *Arrived*. Thus the relationship between a grandfather, who is a ›philosopher‹, and his grandson, who is a successful ›dramatic writer‹, also becomes a theme. ‹The grandchildren have everything from their maternal grandfathers‹, is what he has his ›mother‹ character say (S II/378). Her guest, on the other hand, formulates a criterion for the quality of work of a writer, which immediately makes us think of Bernhard's grandfather, who was unsuccessful for most of his life:

We only have evidence of the failure
of the writer
All writers have failed
there have only ever been failed writers [...]
they all assume
that they fail
when they are valued

(St III/355)

Only a year later, Bernhard's readers could once again see the analogy in connection with Freumbichler. In his autobiographical volume *A Child* he says, ›He always had the most incredible ideas, but he always felt that these ideas were the cause of his failure.‹ It is this quality which is so forcibly associated with the writer, Johannes Freumbichler, as a person. Again, the narrator places himself in the same line of tradition – as in the example given above of the image of the world as a cesspit, here he identifies with the philosophy of life attributed to his grandfather: ›We all fail, he said time and again. That is the thought that most occupies my mind, too.‹ (GE 52)

In some respects Bernhard's play *Der Theatermacher* (*Histrionics*, 1984) seems to be a continuation of the comedy about the circus director, Caribaldi, written ten years previously. The state-actor, Bruscon, who, as the manager of a troupe of travelling players formed entirely by members of his own family, tries to give mankind a ›historical diatribe‹ (Hi 278), by using theatrical means. He too recites the same catalogue of pretensions that we have already heard from Caribaldi:

Only because we believe in ourselves
do we manage to endure it [...]
because we believe in our art [...]
Nothing else interests us
but our art
nothing more [...]
Stop at nothing of course

(Hi 274)

›What is the worst thing for a creative person? – To doubt your own work!!‹, is what Freumbichler wrote in one of his notebooks around 1943/44. ›What eliminates this: the healthy belief, to the point of doggedness, in having created something truly great.‹ On the one hand *Histrionics* is also about the failure of high-flying artistic ideas, in the face of a world hostile to art, a bitter parody on the classic project of the ›stage as a moral institution‹ (Friedrich Schiller). On the other hand, the old family-play which the young Thomas Bernhard had taken part in as a child becomes visible again behind the scenes. This time the author even has his protagonist ironically allude to his dependence on his grandfather's identity when he speaks of his ›cap of advantage‹ that he inherited from his maternal grandfather. ›If I wanted to think I would put this cap on,‹ he says to the landlord of a run-down pub in which the play takes place. ›And just imagine / I simply couldn't manage to think even in the city / without that linen cap of my grandfather's‹ (Hi 195). From this passage it becomes especially evident, to what extent Bernhard plays with elements from his own life in his literary work when they have become the basis for his fictional writing. For all the features of the grandfather that Bruscon bears he is not a pure Freumbichler-character – after all, the author puts statements in his mouth which obviously de-scribe the grandfather-grandson relationship from the *grandson's* perspective.

›My grandfather's good nature had its limits and, as far as his work was concerned, he knew no mercy, and we were often made to feel his absolute tyranny,‹ writes Bernard in his autobiographical volume *The Cellar*. ›He was capable at times of positively devastating hardness and asperity, especially towards the women – his wife and daughter‹ (GE 185). This, apart from the hostile society already encountered on several occasions, touches on a second larger area of the imagination, onto which Bernhard's characters especially like to project their persecution mania: the ›female‹.

Johannes Freumbichler, Traunstein 1938

In *Histrionics* we discover, in a comic variation, what was previously expounded in an aggressive way, especially in Bernhard's prose, mostly in relation to the respective mothers – from *Frost* to *Das Kalkwerk/The Lime Works* (1970), to *Correction* and finally to *Auslöschung/ Extinction* (the novel which was published in 1986, most of which was written before *Histrionics*). Time after time Bruscon utters sentences such as the following:

Women have no concept of art
women have nor idea of anything
philosophical [...]
they try all right
but it's no use
can't be taken seriously

(Hi 252)

›All great hermits, prophets and philosophers are thought of without women – in fact they are unimaginable with a woman,‹ writes Freumbichler in one of his notebooks around 1944/45. It is a theme that occupied his mind at that time (which was the time when his grandson, Thomas Bernhard, reached puberty) more than anything else, as is evident from the number of references to it. ›To a woman the average man is nothing but an object of exploitation, and beyond that at worst nothing,‹ he notes at another point – a despairing, frustrated writer coming to the end of his life during which he had lived mainly from the

Johannes Freumbichler
with his granddaughter,
Susanne Fabjan,
Traunstein around 1941

incomes of his wife and daughter. ›A man senses this and tries, for his part, to enslave her. Thus the deep hatred in a normal marriage, the eternal strife.‹

A point worthy of note is that Bernhard's own treatment of this subject not only varies the grandfather's view of life in literary form, but in its actual development also shows a strange parallel to Freumbichler's reflections. In about 1948 Bernhard's grandfather reached the conclusion, expressed in his notes, that his curious phobia of ›woman‹ was basically the work of projection mechanisms. ›Those men who don't feel comfortable in their own skin have created a devil which they call »woman« and which they endow with the worst qualities in the world.‹ Towards the end of his literary career, Freumbichler's grandson actually has one of his main characters express very similar thoughts. In *Extinction*, Bernhard's protagonist, Franz-Josef Murau, puts in perspective the passionate defamation of his mother, whom he describes (not differently to his literary predecessors Strauch, Konrad and Roithamer) as being the decisive annihilator of his existence in a passage which one can certainly read as also being Bernhard's late comment on the discourse on ›woman‹ of previous texts: ›It would be quite wrong to blame her for all the bad things she's done,‹ admits Murau. ›We do this only because we have no alternative, be-

cause it's too difficult to think differently, too complicated [...]; and so we simplify the matter and say *Our mother is a bad person*, and all our lives we stick to this judgement.‹ (Ex 148)

In one of his prose texts from about the same period as the autobiography Thomas Bernhard once again reproduces the complex game of self-observation and identification with his late grandfather that we have analysed with several examples. The basis of the narrative *Beton* (*Concrete*, 1982) is the writing-blockage felt by Rudolf, the music-critic, who is working on a study of Felix Mendelssohn-Bartholdy. In one of the most impressive passages of the book he tries, once more, to revive his creativity, which has let him down again: ›I had meant to begin working at four o'clock and now it was five. I was alarmed by this negligence of mine, or rather this lack of discipline.‹ Rudolf consequently takes the part of the grandfather, with the help of some actual objects, which, in his autobiography, Bernhard elevated to emblematic components of the image of his grandfather's appearance: ›I got up and wrapped myself in a blanket, the horse blanket I had inherited from my maternal grandfather, and tied it round me as tightly as I could with the leather belt which was also inherited from my grandfather, so tightly that I could scarcely breathe. Then I sat down at my desk.‹ (Co 3)

When even this attempt fails, another step in the change of roles ensues: ›I went upstairs but didn't immediately sit down at my desk. I looked at it through the door of the thirty-foot upstairs room, standing about twenty-five to thirty feet away from it, to see whether everything on it was in order‹ (Co 11f.). By doing this Rudolf literally emerges from himself, becoming an imaginary object of observation: ›I looked steadily at the desk until I could see myself sitting at it, as it were from behind.‹ Seen from a distance in this way, he puts himself again into the existential ›framework‹ which the deceased model has placed at his disposal:

That's the back of my maternal grandfather, I thought, about a year before his death. I have the same posture, I told myself. Without moving I compared my own back with my grandfather's, thinking of a particular photograph that had been taken only a year before his death.

(Co 12)

Soon after this, however, the image vanishes and sobering reality catches up with the writer:

›Then the image vanished. I was no longer sitting at my desk; the desk was empty, and so was the sheet of paper on it.‹ (ibid.) Yet in front of us we have a book about the failure of a writer that demonstrates the ultimate success of its author, Thomas Bernhard – who in his literary career reversed the model of his grandfather ›in the opposite direction‹.

In this essay we did not especially indicate which of Bernhard's texts have actually been translated into English. A list of these translated texts can be found in Bernhard's biography, p. 158f. The other titles are loose translations of the German originals. Quotations from Bernhard's texts were taken from the following translations:

Co *Concrete*, trans. David McLintock. London, New York: Quartet 1989.
Ex *Extinction*, trans. David McLintock. New York: Knopf 1995.
GE *Gathering Evidence. A Memoir*, trans. David McLintock. New York: Vintage 1993.
Hi *Histrionics. Three Plays*, trans. Peter Jansen and Kenneth Northcott. Chicago and London: The University of Chicago Press 1990.
Lo *The Loser*, trans. Jack Dawson. Chicago and London: The University of Chicago Press 1996.

In all other cases the German versions of Bernhard's texts were translated for this essay:

G *Gehen*. Frankfurt am Main: Suhrkamp 1971.
St *Die Stücke*. 4 vols. Frankfurt am Main: Suhrkamp 1988.
TBL *Thomas Bernhard. Ein Lesebuch*, ed. by Raimund Fellinger. Frankfurt am Main: Suhrkamp 1993.

Joseph and Maria
Freumbichler with
their children

Joseph Freumbichler (1830-1909)

Maria Freumbichler (1843-1920)

My greatgrandfather sold dripping
and today
everyone still knows him
between Henndorf and Thalgau
Seekirchen and Köstendorf
and they hear his voice
and move
together at his table
that was also the master's table.
In spring, 1881,
he chose life: he planted
a vine by the wall of the house
and called the beggars together;
his wife, Maria, the one with the black ribbon,
gave him another thousand years.
He invented the music of pigs
and the fire of bitterness,
he spoke of the wind
and of the wedding of the dead.
He wouldn't give me a piece of bacon
for my despair.

The house of
Freumbichler's father
in Henndorf,
Kirchenstraße 14

Thomas Bernhard: *Auf der Erde und in der Hölle/On Earth and in Hell*

23

An elder brother of my grandfather, Rudolf, escaped to the forest and became a forester on Uiberacker estates around the Wallersee and the Mondsee. Here, at the age of thirty-two, he committed suicide because he could no longer bear the misery of the world, as he put it in a handwritten note found beside his body, which was found guarded by his dachshund.

A Child

We admire a man like my uncle, who killed himself because he *could no longer endure the unhappiness of mankind*, as he wrote on the slip of paper they found in his coat pocket, dated by him on the day he threw himself down the air shaft of the cheese factory, because he's ahead of us in having the capacity to commit suicide, not only to talk about committing suicide but to commit suicide in fact, so Roithamer.

Correction

Rudolf Freumbichler (1876-1902),
Johannes Freumbichler's brother

Rudolf Freumbichler's
suicide note

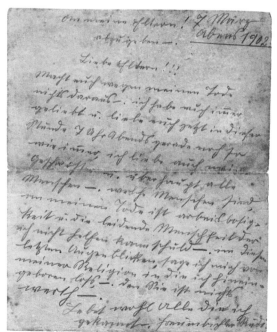

Dear Parents,
Don't worry yourselves about my death. I have always loved you and I still love you as much as ever at this hour, 7 o'clock in the evening, I love my bro-thers and sisters, too, in fact all human beings, who are human. Unemployment and the suffering of mankind that I cannot help are to blame for my death. In these last moments I renounce the re-ligion I was born into -, for it is worth nothing -, Farewell to all those I know.

From Rudolf Freumbichler's suicide note, 7th March 1902

Marie Freumbichler (1875-1952), a sister of Johannes
Freumbichler, married to the painter, Ferdinand Ruß

Fernanda Ruß (1899-1979), her daughter,
married to Said Edip Bey

His elder sister, Marie, had also seen this brainless routine for what it was and decided it was unworthy of her. As a young woman she had married an artist from Eger,
who later became a celebrity in Mexico and is still discussed in the art columns of
the big newspapers. She had a daughter by this painter and spent many years in
the East, dragging her daughter around with her from pasha to pasha, from sheikh
to sheikh, and from bey to bey. Having reached her forties and parted from all her
pashas, sheikhs, and beys, [...] she ended up as a mediocre actress at the Court
Theatre in Vienna.

A Child

Rudolf Kasparek (1885-1920),
Freumbichler's closest friend of their early years

Kasparek´s last letter
to Freumbichler

We should be idealists, you say. But we don't stand and wait around bravely, no
we want the ideals of our dreams that fill our youthful hearts to come true and we
dedicate all our energy to this task. Willingly, willingly my dear friend. Nothing
shall prevent me from stout-heartedly taking part in the making of a home of happiness for the harrassed human race.

The nights are truly tortuous. Mornings exhausting. I don´t feel human again until
somewhere around 11:30, after I´ve been awake awhile and lain on the sofa for a
half-hour. Then, the feeling that I´m not going to make it disappears for a while.
[...]
In a word, it´s too cold here to even die. Best wishes for the time being. I hope
that you´ll write again – and that you´re not suffering from the cold!

Extracts from Rudolf Kasparek's letters to Johannes Freumbichler (1902; last letter from 1919)

HOF-ATELIER SEILING
MÜNCHEN

Johannes Freumbichler,
1910 (the only available
photo of his early years)

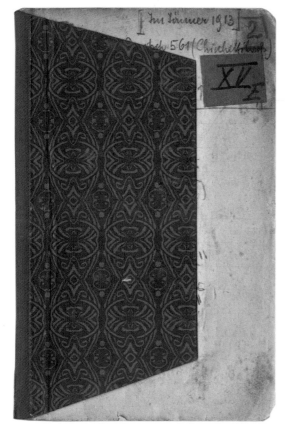

I have something invincible, unconquerable in me,
thus, should the worst arise, I shall not despair, and
go on living....

Anxiety and the misery of poverty,
how long will I go on living like this?
I want to work, to overcome them.

Everyday, as in a kind of madness to continue to
work and reflect on my themes that would save me.

What shall I do? – What shall I do? – What shall I
do? – Why can't I live at the height of humanity???
Where, not to the benefit of a generation, but simply and solely my place is, where I belong?

From Freumbichler's notebooks

Deutsche Romanzeitung
Romanbibliothek

1918   Heft 17

Eduard Aring / Roman von Johannes Freumbichler

1. Kapitel.

Am Fuße der Alpen liegt zwischen sanften, grünen Hügeln und dunkelragenden Hochwäldern das kleine, idyllische Tal Elingheim, durch dessen gesegnete Fluren ein frischer, kristallheller Waldbach sein glänzendes Silberband zieht. Dort, wo das muntere Wässerchen eine Biegung macht und, aus weißleuchtendem Birkenhain kommend, lustig üppiggrüne Matten durchrauscht, winkt das freundliche Dörflein Talham. Die schmucken, weißgetünchten Häuschen und Höfe schmiegen sich an einen sanft ansteigenden Hügel, den ein stattlicher, dem Wanderer schon von ferne in die Augen fallender Hof krönt. Das ist der Aringhof. Ein gewundenes Sträßlein, weißleuchtend im Grün der Anger und Obstgärten, führt zu seinen Vorplatz hinauf. . . .

Ein blauer, wolkenloser Julihimmel strahlte zur Zeit hernieder, und Sommerträume woben über dem Tal. Schon neigte sich das Gestirn gegen die Hochwaldkämme, und die Buchen- und Birkenwäldchen, die in der Gegend anmutig zerstreut liegen, waren mit rosigen Lichtfluten übergossen. Getreide, in der goldenen Farbe des Reifens, wogte im purpurnen Abendscheine, die Wiesen, mit Blumen durchwirkt, leuchteten grünsamten, und die schmalen Streifen der Flachsfelder schimmerten hell. Stille lagen Tal und Dorf. Still und verlassen lag auch auf dem Hügel der Aringhof, und nichts ließ sich hören, als das Plätschern des laufenden Brunnens, der seinen klaren Strahl in monotoner Melodie in einen grünbemoosten, hohlen Baumstamm fallen ließ, und das gedämpfte Gezwitscher der Schwalben, die bei den offenen Kammerfenstern des Obergeschosses

geschäftig aus- und einflogen. Das hellgrüne Laub der Birnbäume, die an den Wandspalieren ihre Zweige ausbreiteten, zitterte leicht im Winde. In den kleinen, vergitterten Fensterchen blühten buntfarbige Fuchsien und Pelargonien. In den eisernen Fensterkreuzen staken Büschel von Johanneskraut, das, einem alten Glauben zufolge, bösen Geistern den Eintritt ins Haus verwehrte. . .

Undeutliche Stimmen, die aus dem Hause kamen, und dann helles, übermütiges Mädchenlachen unterbrachen die Stille. Im nächsten Augenblicke trat eine stattliche Frau in ländlicher Sommertracht vors Haus und blickte, die Hand über die Augen haltend, aufs Dorf hinab. Das war die muntere, rührige Magdalena, die Herrin am Aringhof. Sie ließ suchend ihre Blicke über Felder und Wiesen schweifen, wo sie überall emsig arbeitende Landleute bemerkte, und dort, links vom Birkenwäldchen, auch die Leute vom Aringhof. Prüfend beobachtete sie dann eine Weile den Himmel. Endlich wandte sie sich und rief ins Haus: „Heh! Guste! Mach' flink! — Bring' die Klapper! — Sie sollen Feierabend machen!"

Von drinnen antwortete eine helle Mädchenstimme: „Gleich komm' ich, Base! Gleich!"

Magda trat zur Hausbank, wo eine Reihe frischgescheuerter Zinngeschirre aufgestellt waren, und wandte eins nach dem andern der Sonne zu. Sie glänzten und gleißten, als wären sie eitel Silber.

Da kam auch schon ein junges, nußbraunes Mädchen trällernd aus dem Hause und lief geschäftig zum Anger vor. Frau Magda sah dem hübschen Kinde lächelnd nach und betrachtete wohlgefällig die frischen, roten Wangen, den

Anna Bernhard
(presumably the rest of her wedding photo; she had
left her husband and children to follow Freumbichler)

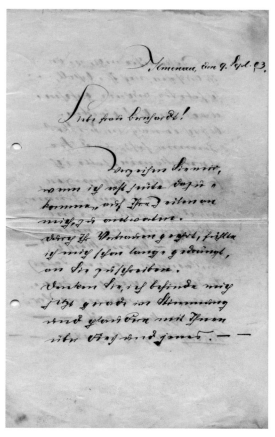

Johannes Freumbichler's first letter
to Anna Bernhard (Ilmenau, 9.9.1903)

Not only you, but the female sex in general, is in
wretched servitude, in slavery.

Everywhere woman is the slave of the roughest
and most callous man. Wherever you look you can
see this humiliation, this shameful state, and it is
only outwardly less apparent because, after a thousand years of servitude and humility, most women
have sunk into slavery.

[...] The more independent ones try to escape, to
free themselves from the wretched state they find
themselves in, having been sold off by their
parents for the sake of financial gain. – A great
movement has been formed, the emancipation of
women or the freedom of women, whose purpose
is to give women back their freedom and happiness.

From Freumbichler's first letter to Anna Bernhard

Werinhart [=Johannes] Freumbichler is now my
friend, my dear friend, oh, I thank you, and at the
same time ask you to make do with my humble
self, perhaps you may even love me a little. When I
first saw you, I thought to myself: he's a bit of an
eccentric, excuse me for using that expression but
I prefer to tell the truth.

Dear friend, my dear Tuisko tells me you are suffering. My God, I feel so sorry for you. I would think
myself lucky to be allowed to take care of you, or
do you any kind of service.

From Anna Bernhard's first letter
to Johannes Freumbichler (Salzburg, Sept. 1903)

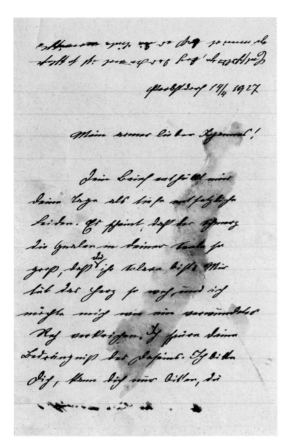

A letter from Anna Bernhard
to Johannes Freumbichler (1927)

SECESSIONS-FORMAT
G·PICHLER   D-HALLEIN.

Anna Bernhard

You must not give up hope, the day must come for you,
too, when you will be freed from the dark night of prison. I
think you brood too much. If you throw away your valuable
life people will say sympathetically, oh well, he was a
weakling. Should we really have suffered so much for that
final result? [...] It will come to light who you are.

You mistrust women so much that you hardly manage to
feel appreciation, let alone high esteem. I can only say,
dear friend, that you often do me an injustice. You don't
think I am able to care for you, otherwise you would believe me when I say that I had no peace day and night.
The thought that all feelings are answered with mistrust
makes me think that you are weary of me.

From Anna Bernhard's letters to Johannes Freumbichler, Vienna (1927)

Letter from Anna Bernhard
to Johannes Freumbichler (1927)

Anna Bernhard
in nurse's uniform

An artist's wife must also be a genius and unite a dozen women in one. You have to be able to hide it when you go to him needing affection and he surrounds himself with a wall of indifference. It hurts, you feel helpless, insignificant. An artist only loves his art and that makes him an egotist. A noble egotist. [...] You have to let him do what he wants, without asking the reason why. Expect nothing, give everything, sit quietly when he gives in to his moods, and be enthusiastic during his bright times. Above all, love him from the bottom of your heart, with all that, and eliminate yourself.

From Anna Bernhard's letter (repr. above)

Anna Bernhard
as a nanny

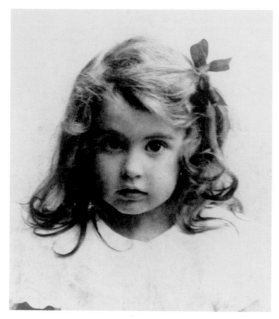

Herta Bernhard as a child

His life-long companion, who later became my grandmother, had been forced by her parents into a terrible marriage, which lasted for years, with a Salzburg tailor. She eventually left her husband and two children and went to Basel, where she fell on my grandfather's neck and swore to stay with him forever, no matter where. So it happened that my mother was born in Basel. She was a beautiful child and remained a beauty all her life.

A Child

Herta Bernhard,
1920s

My dear, good father!

Sunday, and I'm so alone and feel like writing something nice to you, but if you're sad I'm sad too, it just seemed to me as if the two of us together were one person who has to live or perish. I already regret spending Thursday in such stupid company, but with you, even if you don't laugh it's much nicer, everytime I feel I have learned something.

Letter from Herta Bernhard
to Johannes Freumbichler (Vienna, 1927)

Herta Bernhard,
1920s

Anna Bernhard with
her grandson Thomas,
Vienna 1934

Alois Zuckerstätter (1905-1940),
Thomas Bernhard's father

Herta Bernhard with Thomas, Vienna 1933

It was a portrait of my father, and it was so like me
that I had a fright.

In the Cold

Monday, 9 a.m. I got the first shock, the pains were
not so bad at that point, it wasn't until 3 o'clock in
the afternoon that the labour pains became really
bad and so it went on until 8p.m. when little Tommy
appeared at last, I heard a clap and at the same
time a little voice, and Tommy came to life.

Letter from Herta Bernhard
to her parents, Heerlen 1931

Herta Bernhard with her husband-to-be, Emil Fabjan,
mid-1930s

Thomas Bernhard with his mother, Seekirchen 1936

I spent more time with my grandfather than with my mother, with whom my relations were always difficult, ultimately because she found my very existence incomprehensible and was never able to come to terms with it. [...]. I always found it extremely difficult to live with my mother, *whose nature I am to this day quite unable to describe*. I cannot give an indication of her character, and even today I find it impossible *to comprehend even approximately* the eventful life she led, which came to an end when she was only forty-six. [...] I spent more time with my grandparents than with my mother, for it was with them that I found all the love, affection, and understanding I could find nowhere else.

An Indication of the Cause

Johannes Freumbichler
and his grandson
Thomas Bernhard,
Seekirchen 1937

My dear Grandfather!
I and Mummy wish you for your birthday above all
health, success and a long, better life!
Yours, Thomas

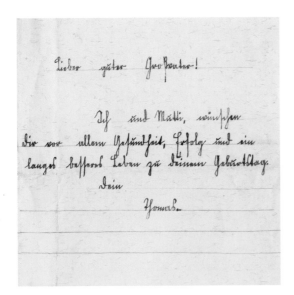

Drawings of little Thomas Bernhard –
the first scenes for the theatre!

Thomas Bernhard, his Uncle ›Farald‹, and his grandparents, Seekirchen 1936

My grandfather, whom I loved more than anyone else in the world, suddenly became the city gentleman with the walking stick, who was regarded by everybody with curiosity but also with suspicion – a novelist, a thinker! The contempt he attracted outweighed the admiration. This gentleman could not even afford to take his meals in the parlour. Other people went to work; he went for walks. My grandmother got a job at Hipping Farm, high above Seekirchen [...]. She earned enough to keep us.

A Child

Anna Freumbichler with Peter Fabjan, Emil and Herta Fabjan, Thomas Bernhard,
Johannes Freumbichler (at the back), Ettendorf/Traunstein 1938

To this extent we were a circus family of tightrope
walkers who never for one moment allowed themselves to get off the rope, and our act became daily
more difficult to perform. We were prisoners of the
tightrope, exponents of the art of survival; below us
lay normality, but we dared not plunge into it,
because this, we knew, would have meant certain
death.

A Child

Johannes and Anna
Freumbichler,
Traunstein 1938

All hope was now concentrated not on Traunstein but on a famous author who lived nearby, in my grandparents' home village of Henndorf. I was given to understand that my grandmother had taken a manuscript to the famous man, who was trying to find a publisher for it. [...] The world of these famous people seemed to me quite sensational. As the celebrities arrived, alighted from their cars, and walked up the garden, we children watched in admiration through the upper window of the log hut. Famous actors, writers, sculptors – in fact, artists and intellectuals of all kinds – went in and out of the house. The famous writer was completely different from my grandfather, who, though of course he was also a writer, was not at all famous.

A Child

Carl and Alice Zuckmayer in Henndorf

Carl Zuckmayer's first letter to Anna Bernhard (written on Freumbichler's birthday!)

One of Freumbichler's notebooks containing a working schedule for his novel, *Philomena Ellenhub* (10 pages per day)

Advertisement for Freumbichler's novel, *Philomena Ellenhub* (publ. 1937)

Telegram announcing that the novel would be published

One day a telegram arrived, informing my grandfather that his novel had been accepted by a publisher in Vienna. The famous man had been as good as his word. The book was published, and my grandfather got a national prize for it. The first and only success had been achieved. My grandfather was fifty-six.

A Child

44

Johannes Freumbichler,
Traunstein

Feuilleton.

Ein Salzburger Bauernroman.

Wenn ich versuche, von diesem wunderbaren Buch, „Philomena Ellenhub" — dem Salzburger Bauernroman von Johannes Freumbichler — zu berichten, wahrhaft wunderbar als Erscheinung wie als Werk — so heißt es fast: von einem lebendigen Menschen zu erzählen, den man lange und gut gekannt hat, — oder von einer Welt voll gegenwärtiger und unverlierbarer Gestalten, wie sie uns immer wieder in einer wohlvertrauten Landschaft begegnen. Der einfache Lebensweg einer Bauernmagd, umrankt vom vielfältigen Wuchs des ländlichen, dörflichen, bäuerischen Daseins, wird hier — ohne Vorsatz oder Absicht, nur durch die schlichte Formung seiner Wahrheit und Wirklichkeit — zum Sinnbild des irdischen Lebens überhaupt, — die Menschen, die sich in ihrer Lebensnot und -lust, in ihrem simpelsten Alltag und in ihrer heimlichen, abwegigen Verzauberung enthüllen, tragen das Zeichen ihrer ewigen Bestimmung an der Stirn — und die Landschaft, darin sie leben und atmen, stets vom Geheimnis des Wechsels und Wandels umwittert, vom Hauch des Schöpferatems durchweht, vom Himmel der Träume und Ahnungen überwölbt — wächst zur Landschaft der Seele.

Es sei gleich gesagt: dieser „Salzburger Bauernroman" des Johannes Freumbichler (Paul Zsolnay Verlag, Wien) hat mit Bauerndichtung im üblichen beschränkten Sinne ebensowenig zu tun, wie etwa ein Werk von Stifter oder Hamsun. Man findet hier nichts von der hausbackenen Realistik, noch weniger von der falschen Verzierung und Schönfärberei, von der philiströsen und glatten Eingängigkeit, die dem Begriff „Heimatkunst" den Beigeschmack von Enge und Bierstüberlniveau verliehen hat, — und am allerwenigsten ist diese wahrhaft ursprüngliche, im höchsten Sinn einfältige und volksverbundene Erzählung irgendeiner schlagworthaft zeitgemäßen Programmatik einzuordnen. Ich halte dieses Buch für eine in seiner Art wirklich ganz ungewöhnliche und einzigartige Erscheinung, denn es ist vollkommen ohne Vorbild, vollkommen „unliterarisch", und dabei vollkommen dichterisch. Hier erzählt ein Mensch, dem das Wort gegeben ist, zu sagen und zu künden, und der die Welt seiner nächsten unmittelbaren Anschauung, das Ueberkommene, Gelebte und Erfahrene, — in seiner wahrheits- und sinnverschworenen, ebenso liebreichen wie rücksichtslos unverhohlenen Wiederschöpfung zum Weltganzen erhebt. Daß diese Welt gerade die unsere, die unserem Herzen verwandteste, die österreichische, die salzburgische ist, und daß der Lebensstand, der sie erfüllt und bevölkert, das unvergängliche, zeitlose, ewig alte und stets

aus sich selbst verjüngte Bauerntum darstellt, — macht das Buch zu einem beglückenden und unverhofften Geschenk.

Ja, es ist wirklich ein klarer Quell, ein lauteres Wasser, ein Himmel voll Sonne, voll Wolkenzug und voll nächtiger Finsternis, voll Wetterleuchten und voll Sternenmilde — gütig, reif und weise, — auch streng, hart und ohne falsche Barmherzigkeit, Rücksicht oder Verhüllung — wahrhaftig bis ins Innerste und doch stets von einer heimlichen Harmonie verklärt, von einer unsichtbaren Waage ausgewichtet, — von seinem eigenen, unbewußten Formgesetz gebaut und getragen.

Es ist die Lebensarbeit eines reifen Mannes, der, von Bauern stammend, zum Dichter berufen, sein ganzes Dasein nur dieser Berufung widmete, ohne doch je den Zugang zur Oeffentlichkeit, zum Widerhall, zum Erfolg gefunden zu haben.

Er, der keiner Härte, keiner Bitternis und keiner Grausamkeit des Daseins aus dem Weg ging, weder in seinem Werk noch in seiner Existenz, vermag es, am Ende dieses Buches das Wort zu sagen: „Erhebet eure Herzen und glaubet daran: Das Leben ist einfach, liebreich und gut."

Carl Zuckmayer.

Carl Zuckmayer's review on *Philomena Ellenhub*,
›Neue Freie Presse‹, 11.2.1937 (this was to become the day of Freumbichler's death, 12 years afterwards)

46

Freumbichler's visiting card

Austrian State Prize Certificate

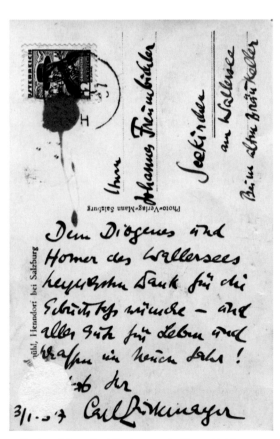

Postcard from Carl Zuckmayer to Freumbichler:
›To the Diogenes und Homer of the Wallersee [...]‹

Haus Wiesmühl
(where the Zuckmayer family lived)

Anna and Johannes Freumbichler, Traunstein

I watched him fondly while he wrote, my grandmother keeping out of his way and quietly calling
us to breakfast, dinner, and supper. Being quiet so
as not to disturb my grandfather became a regular
discipline in the house; while he was alive, quiet
was the supreme requirement. Everything had to
be spoken quietly; we had to walk quietly and always converse quietly. The head is as fragile as an
egg, my grandfather used to say. I saw that this
was so and was shaken by the thought.

A Child

Johannes Freumbichler

Anna Freumbichler

Marriage Certificate of
Johannes and Anna Freumbichler

On my birthday, to my dear Hans. [...]
You may at least be glad to know that you have
given someone who was freezing cold a place in
the sun. You brought me to life and took me into
your school.
They were hard years and our path through life
together was a very stony one.
[...] May God let me go a short way with you still,
then I should be, and shall be grateful. Just one
more thing: When you bury me and cover me with
oblivion you should not forget me, that would be
my immortality. Living at your side I have enjoyed
all the happiness a woman can wish for.

Letter from Anna Freumbichler to her husband, 20.6.1946

Johannes Freumbichler

Towards midday, I would catch sight of my grandfather in the distance and run across the field to
him. In summer he was always dressed in linen
clothes and wearing a panama hat. He never
walked without a stick. We understood each other.
Just a few yards in his company and I was saved.

A Child

Atahuala
oder die Suche nach einem Verschollenen
(novel, publ. 1938)

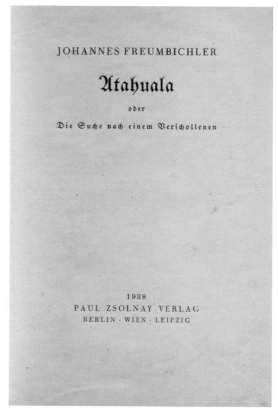

JOHANNES FREUMBICHLER

Atahuala

oder

Die Suche nach einem Verschollenen

1938
PAUL ZSOLNAY VERLAG
BERLIN · WIEN · LEIPZIG

Johannes Freumbichler
in front of the ›Mirtlbauernhäusl‹, Seekirchen around 1936

PAUL ZSOLNAY VERLAG

AKTIENGESELLSCHAFT   GES. M. B. H.
WIEN IV.   BERLIN W 35
PRINZ EUGENSTRASSE 30   POTSDAMERSTRASSE 122
TELEPHON: U-46-5-50 SERIE   TELEPHON: KURFÜRST 5456
TELEGR.: ZSOLNAYVERLAG WIEN   TELEGR.: ZSOLNAYVERLAG BERLIN
BANK: ZENTR.EUROP.LÄNDERB., WIEN   REICHS-KREDIT-ANSTALT A.G., BERLIN
POSTSCHECKKONTI WIEN: WIEN D 9400 · BERLIN 122.838 · BUDAPEST 54.965
PRAG 78.422 · ZAGREB 40.534 · WARSCHAU 195.805 · ZÜRICH VIII 11.119
POSTSCHECKKONTO BERLIN: BERLIN 41.044

Dr.L./Ha   Wien, 25. Juni 1938

Hochverehrter Herr Freumbichler !

    Entschuldigen Sie zunächst bitte, dass wir Ihnen erst heute auf Ihre beiden Schreiben vom Mai l. J. Antwort geben. Wir haben uns jedoch sofort nach Eintreffen Ihres Manuskriptes mit diesem befasst und es von verschiedenen Herren unseres Verlages lesen lassen. Leider herrscht über das Ms durchaus keine einheitliche Meinung. Zwar ist man sich wie das bei Ihnen, hochverehrter Herr Freumbichler, ja selbstverständlich ist, völlig einig über die literarische Bedeutung und die stilistischen Schönheiten Ihres neuen Werkes. Doch glauben wir eine ganze Reihe von Stellen, die uns in einer Zeit wie der heutigen, in der man von jedem Schriftsteller gewisse Stellungnahmen zu weltanschaulichen Problemen als abwegig betrachtet, als für den Vertrieb des Werkes schädlich ansehen zu müssen. Wenn z.B. gesagt wird, " dass aus der Vermishhung der Rassen nicht nur die intelligentesten sondern auch die apartesten Menschenkinder hervorzugehen pflegen " so ist das zweifellos eine Stellungnahme zu einem Thema über das im heutigen Deutschland nicht mehr diskutiert werden kann. Ferner scheinen uns viele Aussprüche des Professors Adamas über den Wert und die Bedeutung des Menschen in Widerspruch zur Auffassung, die heute von kultureller staatspolitisch führender Seite gefordert wird, zu stehen.

    Auch die Meinungen des Paters Benedikt scheinen uns, selbst wenn sie im Wechselgespräch mit dem Maler Ruhland besonders zugespitzt sein müssen, doch manchmal sehr eindeutig (z.B. Muttergottes Bild Seite 312 usw.) Wir wollen Ihnen, hochverehrter Herr Freumbichler, gewiss nicht mit Vorschriften und Hinweisen, die Ihre künstlerische Gesamtkonzeption stören, kommen, aber wir halten es für notwendig, Sie im eigenen Interesse auf diese Punkte aufmerksam zu machen, ehe das Buch dadurch Schaden leiden könnte.

A letter from the Paul Zsolnay publishing company to Johannes Freumbichler

[...] However, there are many passages which must be considered harmful for the distribution of this work when, at times like the present, certain statements by any writer on ideological problems are regarded as erroneous. When, for example, it says ›that not only the most intelligent but also the most striking creatures are usually the result of a mixture of races‹, this is, without doubt a statement on a subject that can no longer be discussed in the Germany of today.

Freumbichlers writing desk, Traunstein 1943

Every morning at three o'clock my grandfather made a fresh start on *The Valley of the Seven Courts*, which he planned as a book of one thousand five hundred manuscript pages. For years now the need to press on with this task had got him up at three o'clock to resume the struggle with death. Debilitated all his life by a serious lung condition, he had made it his custom to start the day at three in the morning by addressing himself to the terrible task that faces the fanatical writer and philosopher, wrapping himself in his horse-blanket and fastening it round his body with an old leather belt. [...] I admired my grandfather's toughness, tenacity, and tireless energy as he wrestled with all the thoughts he had written down and those he had not, because I admired everything about him; yet at the same time I was aware of the truly terrifying madness in which a man like my grandfather must have landed himself, and of the furious speed at which he was inevitably driving his life into a human and philosophical cul-de-sac.

The Cellar

From a notebook on *Jodok Fink*

*Auszug und Heimkehr
des Jodok Fink*
(novel, publ. 1942)

I have 8 finished manuscripts, how could I despair:

1) Salzb. Spinnstub. Gesch.

2) Montbrison

3) I am alone

4) Ljubica

5) Eling

6) Adelholzen

7) Salzburger Gedichte

8) Erz. z. V. u. Fröhlichkeit

From one of Freumbichler's latest notebooks

53

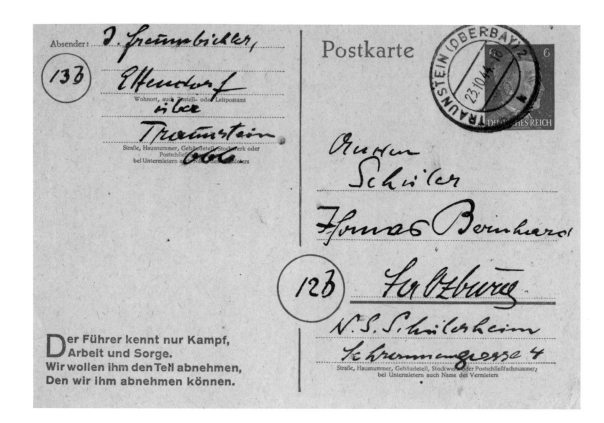

Absender: J. Freumbichler,

(13b)

Ettendorf
über
Traunstein

Der Führer kennt nur Kampf,
Arbeit und Sorge.
Wir wollen ihm den Teil abnehmen,
Den wir ihm abnehmen können.

Postkarte

Meinem
Schüler

Thomas Bernhard

(12b) Salzburg

N.S. Schülerheim
Schrannengasse 4

---

20. September 1944.

Liebster Thomas !
Es war sehr klug von dir ,dass du mir den Brief
des Konzertmeisters gleich gesandt hast.Wir werden
nach dem 15.hingehen und ich hoffe,dass wir
in ihm einen tüchtigen Lehrer für dich bekommen
werden.Es ist heute nötig,dass sich ein junger
Mensch auf vielen Gebieten ausbildet.Habt Jhr in
der 2.ten englisch?-Wenn nicht,so muss auch hier
Privatunterricht genommen werden..Lerne
fleissig!-Dein späteres Lebensglück baut sich
aus dem auf, was du gelernt hast.Jch bin im
63 Jahr und sitze jeden Tag schon um 4 Uhr
früh am Schreibtisch.Und jetzt tausend
Grüsse   von deinem

Grossvater

J. Freumbichler

Thomas Bernhard and Johannes Freumbichler, Traunstein 1941

Dearest Thomas!
It was wise of you to send me the letter from the
impresario straight away. We will go there after the
15th and I hope we will get a good teacher for you.
Nowadays it is necessary for a young person to get
an education in many subjects. Do you have
English in the second year? – If not, then you will
have to take private lessons. Study hard! Your future happiness in life depends on what you have
learnt. I am in my 63rd and sit at my desk at 4 a.m.
every day.

Postcard from Johannes Freumbichler to his grandson (repr. on p. 54)

From one of Freumbichler's notebooks (with a photo of Thomas Bernhard)

November 1945

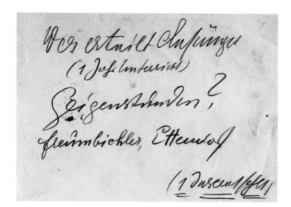

It was undoubtedly my grandfather's wish to make an artist of me; the fact that I was *artistic* misled him into setting himself the aim of turning me into an *artist*. Loving his grandson as he did – and having that love fully reciprocated as long as he lived – he tried every means he knew to turn me into an artist [...].

An Indication of the Cause

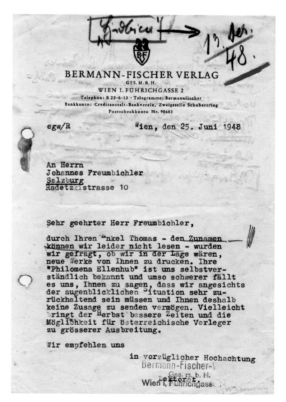

Letter from a publishing company proving that Thomas Bernhard tried to help his grandfather even in his early years

56

Thomas Bernhard

Johannes Freumbichler,
Ettendorf 1940

Johannes Freumbichler's grave in
Maxglan Cemetery, Salzburg

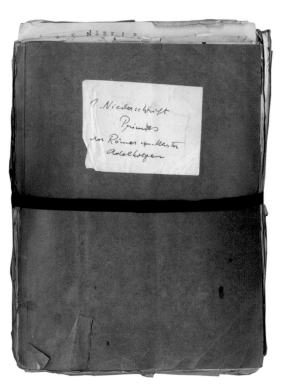

Unpublished manuscripts by Freumbichler

My grandfather lay in state at the cemetery in Maxglan, but was refused burial by the parish priest on the grounds that he had not been married in church. His widow and son (my grandmother and uncle) went to all possible lengths to arrange a burial in the Maxglan cemetery, where he was officially entitled to be buried and where he had wished to be buried, but permission was refused. [...] Finally my uncle, his son, went to see the archbishop and told hit that as he did not know what to do with my grandfather's body – which was now in an advanced state of decomposition after being refused burial by all the Catholic cemeteries in the city – he was going to place it in front of the door of the archbishop's palace. Only then did the Archbishop give permission for my grandfather to be buried at Maxglan.

An Indication of the Cause

59

Anna Freumbichler and Thomas Bernhard, Traunstein 1945

One of Thomas Bernhard´s early notebooks,
following his grandfathers model

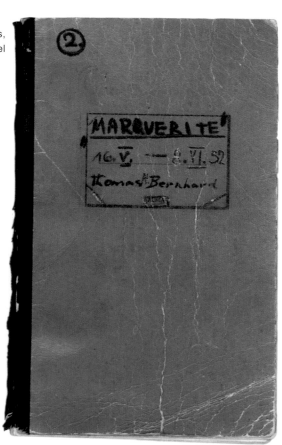

My grandfather's death, though it was a terrible
shock and affected me deeply, was in a sense a
liberation. For the first time in my life I was free,
and I began to take advantage of my new-found
freedom in a way which, as I now realize, was to
save my life [...] A second existence was beckon-
ing to me, a new life of total self-reliance. It is possible – it is even probable – that I knew I owed this
new opportunity solely to my grandfather's death. I
will not elaborate on such speculations.

Breath

60

Personen:

Peter Kühn
ein deutscher Knabe: ——————————

Hans Ellenhub: ——————————

Pielze ⎱ zwei deutsche Heimkehrer
Otto ⎰

ein amerik. Offizier.

——————————

Ort: Berlin 1945

2. Akt
in einem bayrischen Gebirgsdorf
ein Jahr später.

Johannes Freumbichler   1, Akt

In einem Berliner Bahnhofswartesaal.
Es ist kalt, düster, der Morgen bricht an.
In der rechten Ecke sitzt ein etwa 13 jähriger
Junge, schlecht gekleidet, namens Peter Kühn. Er schläft
und ist über den Tisch gebeugt. Züge fahren vor —
über, plötzlich träumt.

Peter: Mutter! — Mutter! — Bist du bei mir?
(er erwacht.)

Pages from an early manuscript by Bernhard, a drama with Peter [i.e. the name of his brother] Kühn and Hans Ellenhub [cf. *Philomena Ellenhub*] as protagonists – written on his grandfather's paper

Anna Bernhard, Peter and Emil Fabjan, Thomas Bernhard, Mayrwies/Salzburg 1951

Unveiling of a memorial tablet at Freumbichler's birth place in Henndorf (1951)

On a beautiful summer's day I was walking through the idyllic cemetery in Maxglan [...]. On an apparently forgotten grave I read the name of a quiet thinker and unique poet who, as I remembered, had been buried there one and half years previously. I thought at once of people wearing the local Henndorf costume, of farmers and farmers' wives with their heads bowed, following the simple coffin. Once more I felt the loss of that great man from the nearby village of Henndorf and as if from afar the songs of praise from his poems rushed into my mind and I saw the characters from his immortal *Philomena Ellenhub.*

Niklas van Heerlen, i.e. Thomas Bernhard:
Vor eines Dichters Grab/At a Poet's Grave, 1950

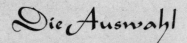

Die Auswahl

AUS DEM LITERARISCHEN SCHAFFEN
DER GEGENWART

Johannes Freumbichler

. . . FÜR ZEIT UND EWIGKEIT VERLASSEN

Konrad saß verblüfft. Ein Werkzeug Gottes? Heute? Er erinnerte sich der qualvollen Entmutigungen im Hofkabinett, der schauerlichen Schwankungen von der höchsten Überzeugung, etwas Außerordentliches hervorzubringen, zu den restlosen Entmutigungen, und es war ihm einen Augenblick zumute, als ob er in einen unerforschten Abgrund hinabblickte, wo sich die Geburt und Wiedergeburt der Schöpfung wie in der Retorte eines Chemikers vollzogen.

„Sie haben vollkommen recht", stimmte Hobian bei. „Die Wortklauberei ist meines Erachtens eine wunderbare Wissenschaft. Man sollte sie pflegen wie das Abc und das Einmaleins. Nehmen wir beispielsweise das Wort armselig. Arm und selig, so hieß es wohl zur Zeit des Urchristentums, als der hohe Geist seines Gründers noch ganz nahe war, als er die Menschen noch unsicher umschwebte, und diese Seligkeit der Armut gibt es wirklich. Sie wundern sich, wie die Seele bei ihrer göttlichen Wesenheit in so grauenvoller Weise ins Böse abirren kann? — Das ist eine Täuschung, sie irrt gar nicht ins Böse ab, sie zieht sich nur, materiell gesprochen, von dem Träger zurück, sie verläßt ihn, und dann ist der Mensch für Zeit und Ewigkeit verlassen. Die Seligkeit der Armut und die Seligkeit der Menschenliebe sind zwei Dinge, die mich seit langem beschäftigen . . ."

Aus dem unveröffentlichten Manuskript
„Das Tal der sieben Höfe"

Ich habe alle Stationen dieses erbarmungswürdigen Lebens durchgemacht, alle Stationen dieser mich täglich rücksichtslos auffressenden Welt. Ich habe diese Welt gespürt wie kein zweiter, ihre Morgen gerochen, ihre Nächte und in der Verzweiflung zurückgefunden zu mir selbst und zu meinen Göttern. Fünfzig Jahre habe ich gebraucht, um zu erkennen, daß es der Hunger ist, der der Schöpfung am nächsten steht, der Hunger einer unabzählbaren Reihe von Generationen, deren Marksteine weit voraus dieser ständig hinuntersinkenden Zeit reichen. Dieser Hunger ist der Erschaffer der Poesien, der Heraufrufer niegesehener Landschaften, der kältesten Nächte, der finstersten Städte, der wasserlosesten Wüsten. Aus diesen kältesten Nächten, aus diesen finstersten Städten, aus diesen wasserlosen Wüsten befreit sich die Dichtung, das, was die gewaltigen Literaturen der Erde ausmacht. Ich sehe mich in diesem Hunger eingekerkert, in dem Hunger meiner Leidenschaften, die von den Phrygern und Römern bis zu den Atemstößen unserer Zeit strömen. Dieser Hunger ist unauslöschlich. Ich werde ihn trinken, solange ich lebe, unaufhörlich werde ich diesen Hunger lieben, denn er allein ist dieses erschütternden und ruhmreichen Daseins Rätsel. *Eine Eintragung aus dem Nachlaß*

11

Thomas Bernhard's attempt at preserving his grandfather's memory:
Together with an original essay on him, he published extracts from Freumbichler's unpublished writings.

Johannes Freumbichler: Biography

1873 Joseph Freumbichler (small shopkeeper, grocer, seller of dripping, ›Schmalz-Sepp‹, 1830-1909) marries his second wife, Maria Langer (1843-1920).

1878 birth of Anna Maria Schönberg in Bad Reichenhall (20.6). Parents: Maria Schönberg, needle-woman, and Johann Pichler, a dealer in animals for slaughter, married 1880; Anna becomes legit. as ›Pichler‹ 1887.

1881 birth of Johannes Freumbichler (Birth Certificate: Freunbichler) in Henndorf (22.10).

1895 enters the Imperial and Royal State Grammar School in Salzburg; lodgings (as later for Thomas Bernhard) at the Catholic Students' Home, Schrannengasse.

1896 marriage of Anna Pichler to Karl Bernhard (tailor's cutter, 1866-1827) in Salzburg (1.10); Children: Karl Bernhard (1897-1981) and Hans Bernhard (1900-1974).

1901 leaves school prematurely. Prior to this became member of the ›Iron Ring‹ student fraternity (CH= Cheruskia), close friend of Rudolf Kasparek (1885-1920; died of lung disease).

1902 plan to train as an officer fails because of Freumbichler's being shortsighted.
Rudolf Freumbichler commits suicide on the Zifanken, near Henndorf (7.3).
Johannes enrols at Technical School in Altenburg (Saxony).

1903 enrols at the High School for Electro-technology in Ilmenau (Thuringien).
Beginning of correspondence between Freumbichler and Anna Bernhard (in whose house friends from the fraternity were tenants). Freumbichler visits Anna Bernhard (Christmas holidays). Escape plan.

1904 Anna Bernhard gets divorced and starts living with Johannes Freumbichler, at first in Basel. Children: Herta Paula Bernhard

(1904-1950), Farald Rudolf Pichler (1905-1906), Rudolf Harald Pichler (called ›Farald‹ in the family, later became legit. as Freumbichler, 1910-1970).

1911 Freumbichler and his family live in Forstenried, near Munich, probably short-term position as editor. Publication of his novel on marriage, *Julia Wiedeland* (for a deposit of 3,000 Marks).

1913 spends time in Bolzano, TB of the lungs cured in early stage. There he meets Clarita Thomsen (1860-1925), who subsequently supports him spiritually and above all financially. Moves to Vienna (at Clarita Thomsen's suggestion).

1914 employed as typist in the municipality of Vienna (until 1916).
Herta receives ballet lessons, in Vienna, at her father's request.

1916 Herta must go to hospital because of her weak lungs.

1923 hospitalized (lung disease).

1925 death of Clarita Thomsen (11.9); loss of helpful patronage. Extreme, recurring poverty; Anna Bernhard works as housekeeper and nanny. Herta Bernhard supports her father with money from her work as a waitress, home-help and cook.

1930 Herta Bernhard meets Alois Zuckerstätter (1905-1940), becomes pregnant, accepted at the maternity clinic in Heerlen (Holland).

1931 birth of Thomas Bernhard in Heerlen (9.2), after a few weeks the child is taken to his grandparents in Vienna, the mother follows soon after.

1935 the Freumbichler family moves to Seekirchen (Salzburg), after several stops they finally move to the Mirtlbauer house. Meets Carl Zuckmayer, as arranged by Anna Bernhard, who secretly sent Freumbichler's novel, *Philomena Ellenhub*, which had been turned down by several publishers, to the author, who is living near Henndorf. Zuckmayer's wife Alice edits the manuscript with Freumbichler.

1936 marriage of Herta Bernhard to Emil Fabjan (1913-1993), hairdresser, later teacher at

vocational school, in Seekirchen (18.8).

1937 publication of *Philomena Ellenhub* by the Viennese publisher, Zsolnay (through Carl Zuckmayer's mediation).
The Fabjan family (with Thomas Berhard) moves to Traunstein (Bavaria), where Emil Fabjan is employed as a hairdresser.
›Austrian State Prize for Literature‹ for *Philomena Ellenhub*.

1938 Freumbichler and Anna Bernhard move to Ettendorf, near Traunstein.
Publication of *Geschichten aus dem Salzburgischen* and the novel, *Atahuala oder die Suche nach einem Verschollenen*, by Zsolnay.
Johannes Freumbichler marries Anna Bernhard (21.11), in Salzburg.

1942 publication of the narrative *Die Reise nach Waldprechting* and of the semi-autobiographical novel *Auszug und Heimkehr des Jodok Fink*.

1946 the two families (Fabjan and Freumbichler) move to Salzburg. The eight of them move into a three-roomed apartment in Radetzky Str. 10 (Freumbichler demands a room to himself).

1949 Freumbichler in Salzburg Hospital (from 15.1 onwards), two days before his grandson.
Death of Freumbichler (11.2, misdiagnosed), at first, refusal for church funeral (Freumbichler had not married in church), then grave of honour of the City of Salzburg (Maxglan Cemetry).

1950 publication of the article *Vor eines Dichters Grab/At a Poet's Grave* by Niklas van Heerlen (then one of Thomas Bernhard's pseudonyms) in ›Salzburger Volksblatt‹ (12.7).
Death of Herta Fabjan in Salzburg (13.10, cause of death: cancer).

1952 publication of Freumbichler's volume of poetry in local dialect: *Rosmarin und Nelken*. The extensive novel, *Eling. Das Tal der sieben Höfe/The Valley of the Seven Courts*, remains unpublished.

1965 death of Anna Bernhard in Salzburg (1.6); buried in the same grave as her husband.

Thomas Bernhard

1931-1989

The photograph reveals only a single grotesque or comic moment, I thought, not the person as he really was more or less all his life. The photograph is a perverse and treacherous falsification. Every photograph – whoever took it, whoever is pictured in it – is a gross violation of human dignity, a monstrous falsification of nature, a base insult to humanity.

The photographs don't disguise or conceal anything but make everything obvious, brutally obvious, I thought, still contemplating the photos. They reveal everything that the people in them wanted to disguise and conceal all their lives. The distortion and mendacity of the photos is actually the truth, I thought. This total defamation is the truth.

Extinction

Thomas Bernhard
(passport photo),
early 1960s

"Hier ist jeder Stein für mich eine Menschengeschichte,"sagt der Maler."Sie
müssen wissen,ich bin diesem Ort verfallen.Alles,jeder Geruch,ist ~~~~~~~
hier an ein Verbrechen gekettet,an eine Misshandlung,an den Krieg,an irgendeinen infamen Zugriff...Wenn das auch alles vom Schnee zugedeckt ist,"sagt
er."Hunderte und tausende Geschwüre,die dauernd aufgehen.Stimmen,die fortwährend schreien.Sie können von Glück reden,dass Sie so jung sind und eigentlich ohne Erfahrung.Der Krieg war zuende,als Sie zu denken anfingen.Sie wissen von Krieg nichts.Sie wissen nichts.Und diese Menschen,die alle auf der
niedrigsten Stufe stehen,oft auf der niedrigsten Charakterstufe,müssen Sie
wissen,diese Menschen sind alle Kronzeugen der grossen Verbrechen.Dazu kommt
,dass einem ja der Blick zerbrechen muss an den Felswänden.Dieses Tal ist
tödlich für jedes Gemüt." Dann sagt er:"Wissen Sie,dass ich irritiere,das
war ja schon immer mein Fundament.Ich irritiere Sie.Ich irritiere Sie,wie
ich schon immer alle irritiert habe.~~~~~~~~~~~~~~~~~~~~Es tut Ihnen weh.
Ich weiss,Sie ersticken oft in meiner Anzüglichkeit.Hier habe ich die Vorstellung der Auflösung alles Lebendigen,Festen,den Geruch/aller Vorstellun-
gen und Gesetze...Und hier,sehen Sie,die Unterhaltungen mit den Menschen,mit
dem Metzger,mit dem Pfarrer,mit dem Gendarmen,mit dem Lehrer,mit diesem Woll-
kappenmensch...mit diesem typischen Milchtrinker,der,was er sagt,vorher ver-
stümmelt hat,mit diesem fürchterlichen Melancholiker.Alle diese Leute haben
ihre Komplexe. Das kann mit frühem Bettnässen zusammenhängen,wissen Sie,mit
den Walzmustern im Kinderzimmer,in dem Zimmer,in welchem man zum erstenmal
die Augen aufmacht.Alle diese eingeschüchterten Köpfe,"sagt er,"landauf,lang-
ab.Der Lehrer erinnert mich an meine Hilfslehrerzeit,da wird mir übel.Gefühls-
kälte,ja,mit den Jahren macht man da eben radikalere Abstriche,fallen die
Schnörkel weg zugunsten einer rustikaleren Ausdrucksweise,zugunsten des Ver-
standes...Und lauter Kriegserlebnisse,müssen Sie wissen,alles,was diese Leute erzählen,handelt vom Krieg..." Alles sei "entsetzt"."Das Leben zieht sich
zurück und der Tod tritt hervor wie ein Berg,schwarz,jäh,unüberwindlich."Er
hätte es ja sogar zu grosser Berühmtheit,zum grossen Aufsehenmachen bringen
können,doch es interessierte ihn nicht."Mein Talent hätte ausgereicht für
die Weltberühmtheit," sagt er."Sie müssen wissen,die Menschen hängen oft
ein ganz kleines Talent an den grossen Rummel und sind berühmt.Raffinessen!
Der Rummel,der grosse Rummel ist es ! Ich blieb so für mich,sah,was der Rummel ist,der grosse Rummel,und wurde nicht populär.~~~~~~~Weil wir davon gesprochen
haben: der Krieg ist ein unausrottbares Erbgut.Der Krieg ist das eigentli-
che Dritte Geschlecht.Verstehen Sie !"Er wolle so bald als möglich wieder
auf die Station hinunter um Zeitungen."Diese Gerüche,"sagt er,"die Gerüche men-
schenunwürdiger Menschen,wissen Sie,der Geruch der Verkommenheit,des Land-
streichertums und der sogenannten grossen Welt,der Geruch des Verlassen-werdens
und des Verlassenseins,des Ankommens und der Verzweiflung des Fortreisen-
müssens,der menschenhungrigen Reiselust,hat mich immer schon angezogen."

›wrote and wrote and wrote‹

First Annotations on Thomas Bernhard's Literary Remains and Method of Working

Martin Huber

The end of the narrative *Die Mütze/The Cap*, quoted in the title, with its perpetuation of the process of writing, breaks through the boundary of the individual text, at the same time leaving it behind as an ›established interim result of the writing process‹ (Hurlebusch 1998, 10). Consequently, it also refers, at least indirectly, to the author's other texts, and finally to his complete literary remains. At the same time it draws attention to the writing process itself, to Thomas Bernhard's method of working.

Both themes – working method and literary remains – already occupy a central position in the published works; the proposition maintained here is that taking a look at both complex themes in Bernhard's work prepares the way towards an understanding of his working method, as can be deduced from the type-written text, thus opening up the approach to his literary remains.

Among the basic recurring constellations in Bernhard's texts is the one in which the prota-

Thomas Bernhard: *Frost*, typed manuscript

gonist has a ›finished‹ study in his head that ›only‹ needs to be put onto paper, which of course he fails to do. A typical example of this type is Konrad in the novel *Das Kalkwerk/The Lime Works*, who, after carrying out a study on hearing which took him years, just is not able to put it down on paper. At the end of the novel in which Konrad's act is reconstructed as a narrative account by a life-assurance agent who questioned Wieser and Fro, two of Konrad's acquaintants (during the night of 24th to 25th December Konrad shot his wife, who was confined to a wheelchair), we find his insight into the reasons for this failure – which of course is too late for the protagonist: that there is no ideal moment for writing something down at all – and that he simply lacked the fearlessness to transfer the study from his head to the paper.

Even if this refers to a scientific study which, according to Konrad, would be sure to become a work of art the moment it was written down, such texts certainly can be read to mean Bernhard's own writing, a counter-model as it were, which by being described is exorcised at the same time. This is because the very description of Konrad's failure to write down his study constitutes Bernhard's text, which we have before us as the ›finished‹ novel *The Lime Works*. It exists because its author – to use one of his terse expressions – went in the opposite direction at a decisive point in time, that is, instead of Konrad's continuous state of planning he chose the practice of writing, however imperfect.

In the fourth of the five autobiographical volumes – *Die Kälte. Eine Isolation/In the Cold* – Bernhard affirms his existence in the very practice of writing. The death of his grandfather, which meant the loss of the most important person he related to, in another respect also had the effect of freeing him to indulge his own writing. He uses the products of his writing – his poems – to almost forcibly throw a bridge to the person with whom he had had

a difficult relationship all his life – his mother. He does this when she is dying and he himself is on the way to Grafenhof, a sanatorium for consumptives, because of his illness. In this apparently hopeless situation writing opens up a perspective for him:

When I took my leave of her before going to Grafenhof, where a new phase of uncertainty was about to begin, I read her a few of my poems. She wept – we both wept. [...] I had already taken refuge in writing. I wrote and wrote, hundreds and hundreds of poems – I don't know how many. I existed only through writing. My grandfather had been a writer, and he was now dead. Now I was entitled to write; now I myself had the chance. This was my goal, and I now had the means to attain it. I threw all my energies into writing, exploiting the whole world by transforming it into poetry. My poems may have been worthless, but to me they meant everything. There was nothing more important in the entire world. I no longer possessed anything but the possibility of writing poetry.

(GE 291)

Irrespective of how highly one rates the stylisation of individual details, writing is convincingly presented as an existential act. For Bernhard it becomes the regularly practised art of self-preservation, self-awareness and self-realisation (cf. Hurlebusch 1998, 11).

Part of the product of his writing has been published; an important part, however, starting with his early poems, mentioned above, is to be found in his unpublished literary remains. And there are prefigurations in the published work for dealing with these literary remains. Perhaps the most obvious is in the novel *Korrektur/Correction*: Roithamer's friend wants to ›sift through and put in order‹ the literary remains left to him in Roithamer's last will and testament – as we are told in the first sentence and which the second chapter is about. Whether or not at least the second part of his intention succeeds is doubtful. After much consideration as to how to get the ›thousands of papers‹ of Roithamer's extensive literary remains out of his rucksack, which was otherwise used only for carrying mountain provisions, without mixing them up even more (on his arrival he had only put the main work – Roithamer's Altensam-text – in the drawer) he finally grabbed the rucksack, whilst on ›the edge of desperation‹, and emptied the contents onto the couch in Höller's garret. Although he realises at once that he should not have done that and describes the scene, holding his hand in front of his mouth, as an ›awfully funny situation‹, afterwards he recklessly stuffs the literary remains into the desk-drawer, which he can then only shut with the help of his knee. Despite his rather inappropriate way of handling literary remains, in another passage he fondly imagines himself acting as editor of an historico-critical publication and is fully aware of the importance of all the preserved material, e.g. as regards the various versions of the Altensam-text.

As to Roithamer's major work, the paper entitled *About Altensam and Everything Connected with Altensam, with Special Attention to the Cone*, which after all contains everything Roithamer ever thought in the most concentrated form and in his most characteristic style, as I perceived at once when it first came into my hands at the hospital, and which is more publishable than anything else he ever wrote, I shall pass it on to his publisher untouched, just as I found it, the first eight-hundred-page draft, and the second three-hundred-page revision of this first draft, and the third version, boiled down to only eighty pages, of the second version, *all three of these versions of Roithamer's handwritten manuscript*, for all three versions belong together, each deriving from the previous one, they compose a whole, an integral whole of over a thousand pages in which everything is equally significant so that even the most minor deletion would reduce it all to nothing, [...] *all this taken together is the complete work* [...].
(Cor 150f.)

It is the aim of the middle section of the exhibition to give an insight into Bernhard's

›whole‹, which here is understood in a limited sense to mean the literary remains at hand, whereby even the available literary remains can only be shown in fragments. In order to make their referential nature regarding the total literary remains under discussion quite clear a brief synopsis describes their history and extent before, on a short imaginary conducted tour through the middle aisle, the first real allusions to individual material should ensue.

After Thomas Bernhard's death in 1989 as a first step, his brother Dr. Peter Fabjan gathered together his literary remains in one place for safe-keeping. The literary remains were spread around Bernhard's various apartments and houses, mostly in Hedwig Stavianicek's apartment in Obkirchergasse, Vienna, and in Bernhard's farmhouse in Nathal. The materials were stored in various drawers and boxes, however there was no systematic order. Because of the state of the literary remains, for example with regard to the published works, one may draw the conclusion that Thomas Bernhard kept a significant part of the material. There is no indication that he systematically destroyed material at any time just as he appears not to have made a systematic collection of all the manuscripts and type-written papers. Following Dr. Peter Fabjan's decision to establish a private Thomas Bernhard Trust and that of the Upper Austrian Provincial Government to put the Stonborough-Wittgenstein Villa on the Toscana Peninsula in Gmunden at their disposal for a Thomas Bernhard archive, the literary remains are expected to be available for research as of autumn 2001. Of the entire contents of the literary remains a part will remain in the private family archive (e.g. private correspondence such as the extensive correspondence between Hedwig Staviancek and Thomas Bernhard and certain private documents etc.). The archive in Gmunden will house some of his collections, for example his collection of newspaper cuttings and the correspondence with publishers and theatres, which will form the central part of the complete literary remains (the exact conditions of use and possible time-limits regarding the correspondence are yet to be determined).

The middle section of the exhibition therefore is, strictly speaking, limited to the literary remains. His published work is shown mainly in the form of the corresponding type-written texts. The number of available type-written texts varies from text to text as does the extent of their completion, the intensity of correction of the individual stages of text and their deviation from the published text, etc. A large number of unpublished texts of considerable size have also been preserved which were mainly written in the period before Bernhard's literary breakthrough with the novel *Frost* in 1963.

Manuscripts and type-written texts from the published as well as unpublished sections of the literary remains are shown in the row of glass-cases in the middle aisle and in selected form in the middle section of the catalogue, whereby, through the juxtaposition of the various stages of development and the presentation of the different correction procedures, Thomas Bernhard's method of working becomes comprehensible. The glass-cases show, in a clockwise direction, Thomas Bernhard's literary remains in more or less chronological order and are linked in total in sixteen sections according to theme.

It starts with the first section on Bernhard's lyric poetry, which forms the crucial point of his early work. As examples of his very early writing the two unpublished poems *Die Königin der Städte/The Queen of the Cities* and *Das Wunderland/Wonderland* have been selected, which – as can be concluded by the date ›1948‹ of another poem in this collection of papers and the remark ›good‹, obviously from Johannes Freumbichler – date from the forties. Looking at them from Bernhard's later work these poems are something of a curiosity

with their glorification of Salzburg and Austria. In their attitude, however, they are quite typical, even of the first published poems, e.g. the Salzburg Sonnets in *Handschreiben der Stifterbibliothek* of 1954. There is an echo, in a negative sense, of these beginnings in the angry tone of his later criticism of Salzburg and Austria. *Aufundabzähllied* – from a collection of unpublished poems of the sixties – is an example, already in lyric poetry, of the explicit way in which he comes to terms with his own biography. His first volume of poetry *Auf der Erde und in der Hölle/On Earth and in Hell*, published in 1957 by Otto Müller in Salzburg, represents his published works of poetry, whereby the copy exhibited of the first edition from Bernhard's literary remains shows fundamental revision. If it is true what can be assumed among other things from the script that the corrections were written in, namely that the corrections were made long after 1957 and long after Bernhard's turning away from lyric poetry (Volker Bohn, the editor of the *Gesammelte Gedichte/Collected Poems* assumes, in his editorial note, that it was not until the eighties), then this may show that he subjected his poems to a radical ›revision‹, but at the same time it also shows that they still interested him, even to the point of his wanting to revise them.

The second unit consists of his short prose texts of which some were first published in the literary periodical *Wort in der Zeit* in 1959, others in the *Insel-Almanach 1964*, and which appeared in book form in 1969 in a selection under the title *Ereignisse/Incidents* (published by ›Literarisches Colloquium Berlin‹). These texts originated between 1957 and 1960, the year in which they were to be published by S. Fischer; apparently, however, they were revised to a certain extent. In 1960 Bernhard withdrew the volume shortly before it was due to be published, not as it says in the blurb in the 1969 edition, because he was working on the novel *Frost* (which he probably did not start until later), but because the publishers evidently objected to these texts. The literary remains contain much more than the published *Ereignisse*, in fact most texts appear in several versions that have been revised to a varying degree. As an example of this, the exhibition shows two versions of one of the most well-known texts – *Eine Maschine/A Machine* –, and of the texts published in book form there are three examples: *Zwei junge Leute/ Two Young People*, *Der Schauspieler/The Actor* and *Der Professor*. Of those published in *Wort in der Zeit* the text *Der Unbekannte/ The Stranger* (which appeared here under the title *Ein Unbekannter*) is exhibited, and of the unpublished texts: *Der Hauptmann/The Captain* and *Der Selbstmörder/The Suicide Victim*.

In the next section his *Gartenspiel für den Besitzer eines Lusthauses in Kärnten/Garden Play for the Owner of a House of Pleasure in Carinthia*, which obviously alludes to Gerhard Lampersberg, is representative of his early, unpublished plays, of which there are a considerable number in the form of short dramas in the literary remains and which mostly originated during the time of Bernhard's visits to Tonhof (1957-1960). In 1960 Bernhard's opera libretto *Köpfe/Heads* was performed for the first time at the ›Theater am Tonhof‹. The

musical arrangement was by Gerhard Lampersberg and it was directed by Herbert Wochinz. On the same evening three short plays: *Die Erfundene/The Invented One*, *Rosa* and *Frühling/Spring* were also performed. There are also various versions of these texts under different titles; as an example of this *Übungsstücke für Schauspielschüler/Practice Pieces for Drama Students* is exhibited, a collection which, apart from the above mentioned, also contains the short dramas *Unterhaltung verschiedener Vögel/Conversations between Various Birds*, *Nachspiel zu Rosa/Epilogue on Rosa*, *Zirkus/Circus* and *Die Galgen/The Gallows* and which Bernhard compiled as *Vorspiele für das Theater am Fleischmarkt/ Preludes for the Theater am Fleischmarkt* for its director Herbert Wochinz.

Der Wald auf der Straße/The Forest in the Street and *Tamsweg* give an insight into Bernhard's experiments with the novel before he wrote *Frost*. The handwritten comments on the title page of the first mentioned (›inflated rubbish‹) documents what he himself later thought of such early attempts. *Tamsweg*, dated 1960, so obviously the later of the two, which Bernhard tried unsuccessfully to get accepted by various publishers, already points

Auf der Erde und in der Hölle/
On Earth and in Hell,
segment from Bernhard's private copy

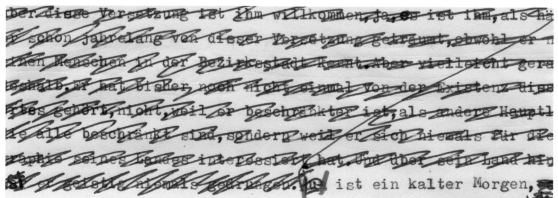

Ereignisse/Incidents, segment from a typed manuscript

in many ways to *Frost*; the exact connections regarding the origin of the texts have yet to be determined. From 1960 we have the fair copy of the extensive novel *Schwarzach St. Veit*; one of the preliminary stages of this novel, dated 1957, clearly shows the transition from lyric poetry to prose as Bernhard used the back of old type-written pages of poetry for writing. The title and place of origin – the novel, as can concluded from a note on the title page, was written in Vienna and Salzburg as well as in St.Veit where Bernhard frequently stayed together with Hedwig Stavianicek – on the one hand refer back to his time at the sanatorium in Grafenhof, and, on the other hand point ahead to the location of the novel *Frost*.

Originally this was planned as the title of a volume of poetry, which suddenly came to him while he was in the cinema – as Bernhard writes during his, in the end, unsuccessful attempts to find a publisher for this volume. The dominating themes – and that was one of the main reasons why the publishers turned him down – were death (*Wo auf den Gräbern der Menschen*), the story of his own family (*Nach meinem Vater frag ich*; *Erinnerung an die tote Mutter, 1931*), frost, as in the title (*Frost* and *Der kommt ins Haus, der Frost*) and finally a new look at Salzburg (*Auf dem Kapuzinerberg*).

As the volume of poetry was never published,

Bernhard could use the title for his first novel, published in 1963. *Frost*, his breakthrough in the literary world, is shown in the exhibition in the form of some examples of the genesis of the text. The literary remains contain one sheet of rough copy, fragments of type-written text, a complete, type-written text and parts of the proofs. The sheet of rough copy still bears the title *Auftrag/Mission*; one can compare the beginning of two versions and the first edition just as one can the ending, which, however, does vary significantly (in the more explicit earlier version Strauch shot himself, in the book version it is mentioned briefly in a newspaper that he has been reported missing).

Bernhard's work and its reception was always connected with public commotion; the scandal at the award ceremony for the ›Austrian State Prize for Literature‹ in 1968 set the trend as it were. In his unpublished prose text *Meine Preise/My Prizes* Bernhard described the prizes awarded to him up to the Büchner Prize and especially the respective award ceremonies, even the stir he caused at the award ceremony for the Austrian State Prize (later Bernhard took up this description again in *Wittgenstein's Nephew*). The speech that caused such a scandal and in whose famous opening sentence it is said that everything is ridiculous when one thinks of death, is enclosed in the type-written text (it was printed in the periodical *Neues Forum* in 1968).

Der Italiener, which first appeared as a prose fragment in *Insel-Almanach* and in *Wort in der Zeit* of 1965 where it was proclaimed by Gerhard Fritsch as a chapter of a book that was still being written, occupies an important place in Bernhard's work in two respects. On the one hand it anticipated the constellation which was later to be fully developed in the big novel *Auslöschung/Extinction*, on the other hand it was Bernhard's first encounter with the film medium, through the TV film *Drei Tage/Three Days* made by Ferry Radax in 1970, in which he succeeded in offering the stage to Bernhard for central statements on his theory of literature. Following this the author rewrote the prose fragment *Der Italiener* as a screenplay for Radax (this is documented by the material exhibited); it was filmed by him in 1971.

Bernhard's breakthrough as a playwright was in connection with Claus Peymann and his first performance of *Ein Fest für Boris/A Party for Boris* in Hamburg in 1970. The play was probably written in 1967 (cf. Dittmar 1990, 117) and should originally have been called *Die Jause/The Snack*. It can be found in the literary remains in some earlier versions which were heavily revised and some of which still have hand-written rough copy on the back of them. All together they illustrate that Bernhard, as with his first novel, also revised his first full-length play intensively.

It was not until 1986, during Claus Peymann's time as director, that Bernhard's plays became a constituent part of the Burgtheater repertoire; however, in 1974 *Die Jagdgesellschaft/ The Hunting Party* was first performed at the Burgtheater. Towards the end of 1974 and the beginning of 1975 there were even talks between the then General Secretary of the Austrian Federal Theatre Association, Robert Jungbluth, and Thomas Bernhard about his taking over the position of manager of the Burgtheater. The Minister for Education, Fred Sinowatz, then decided on Achim Benning – Bernhard assimilated this episode in the typewritten text *Wie ich Burgtheaterdirektor werden sollte/How I was supposed to become manager of the Burgtheater*. Also in 1974, Bernhard's comedy *Die Macht der Gewohnheit/The Force of Habit* was performed for the first time at the Salzburg Festival, directed by Dieter Dorn and with Bernhard Minetti as Caribaldi. The hand-written rough copy that has been preserved shows very well the basic ideas around which Bernhard created his play.

The same is also possible in the case of the material available for the first volume of Bernhard's 5 volume autobiography, *Die Ursache. Eine Andeutung/An Indication of the Cause*. On the sheets of rough copy separate fragments of memory have been recorded, which obviously served him as guide-line while he was actually writing.

As with the *Ursache*, in which the Salzburg priest, Franz Wesenauer, saw himself discre-

Die Ursache/An Indication of the Cause, segment from a draft

nächsten Wochen nützlich und notwendig sein werden und
,diese fünf Bücher auf das Aufmerksamste und mit der in
botenen Langsamkeit zu studieren: Siebenkäs von Jean Paul,
Franz Kafka, ~~Amras von Thomas Bernhard~~ Die Portugiesin
oder Die Anarchie von Broch und dachte jetzt,nachdem ich
ffnet hatte,um besser atmen zu können,dass meine Entschei-
wesen war,Gambetti gerade diese fünf Bücher zu geben und
il sie im Laufe unseres Unterrichts ihm immer wichtiger

Auslöschung/Extinction
segment from the
typed manuscript

dited as ›Onkel Franz‹, there was a legal sequel in the case of the novel *Holzfällen/ Woodcutters* of 1984. Gerhard Lampersberg, who thought he recognised himself as Auersberger in the text, filed an application for the text to be confiscated immediately after publication. The material exhibited of course does not devote itself to this legal question, but documents the findings of the literary remains which are characteristic of his later work. Only rare rough copy still exists or versions which deviate greatly from the published text; the type-written texts are usually corrected in black felt-tipped pen, more extensive changes have been added by corrections over the original.

In the case of his above mentioned last novel *Auslöschung/Extinction* which was published in 1986 but most of which was written in 1981/ 82, there is one single note of rough copy to be found on the envelope containing the instructions for using a washing machine. With regard to the corrections to the type-written texts and the differences to the published text, one correction on the first page is particularly noteworthy, even though it is not easy at first to decipher it because it is marked with black felt-tipped pen. Among the five books Murau set Gambetti to read, *Witiko* by Adalbert Stifter was originally listed instead of *Amras* by Thomas Bernhard.

As far as *Heldenplatz* is concerned, it cannot be about the famous scandal at the Burgtheater premiere in 1988. A sheet of rough copy, which Bernhard evidently used twice, shows how he also first established in writing the ›hot points‹ of his play. The fair copy was chosen precisely from its first pages because – compared, above all, with earlier type-written texts such as the early versions of *Frost* in which the space on one page is used as much as is possible – it shows the sheer wastefulness of the use of pages in his last drama. In the last section there are two projects which Bernhard could no longer complete. The play *Die Schwerhörigen/The Hard of Hearing* had progressed relatively well in comparison with *Neufundland/Newfoundland*, the last novel he had planned. Apart from some pages of rough copy only the first and the last sentences of this novel exist (other titles – *Matterhorn, Karakorum* – either of this novel or other possible texts, are mentioned on a page of rough copy).

The first step towards the classic objective of making use of the material in the literary remains to give a better understanding of the work is to produce an historico-critical edition. First of all, irrespective of the procedure chosen, it represents the attempt ›to document and illustrate as comprehensively as possible‹ the genesis of the texts ›in its complexity from historical, biographical and poetical components‹

76

(Plachta 1997, 14). The focal point – not least with regard to its legibility – is and remains the published text; the documents to do with the origin of a text have been added in a different form.

In contrast, the theory of origin of text-genetics inspired by the French *critique genetique*, meaning the methodical opening up of the process of creation (cf. Hurlebusch 1998, 16), gives the individual texts an autonomous quality. Even if one does not pursue this to the point of proclaiming the equivalence of all stages of text, and one sees the practical difficulty of converting this concept, at least it can be credited with sharpening our view of the evidence of the working process, which is awarded its own standard of expression, and with conditionally enlivening the attempt to achieve a better understanding of the author and his work by shifting the emphasis from the product to the act of producing.

If one starts by roughly dividing authors into those who work in their minds and those who work on paper one soon realises that Thomas Bernhard does not fit easily into either category. However, they may serve as a basis for attempting to place the author in an area which conceives the respective working process more exactly as one that is either ›predominantly reproductive, based on ideas, work-genetic‹ or one that is ›predominantly constructive, self-stimulating, psychogenetic‹ (ibid., 37).

Going back to the studies of Bernhard's work mentioned at the beginning: Protagonists such as Konrad – if they succeeded in their work – would plainly personify the prototype of a head-worker, a reproductive writer for whom everything depends on translating thoughts into writing. Perhaps that is the very reason for their failure. In any case, the method of work of the author who describes this failure is completely different. In the literary remains there are at least some references to ›con-structive‹ elements in Bernhard's method of writing.

Let us take the novel *Frost* as an example. There is a draft in the literary remains but it hardly contains more than a rough structure of the novel and does not come anywhere near e.g. the differentiation of Doderer's construction sketches. In Bernhard's case there is a rough framework but the actual work only results from the practice of writing in intensive phases of work, as for example his brother reports, lasting for some weeks. There are only apparently superficial indications in the type-written scripts of *Frost* that the actual process of working only took place when he was working at his typewriter, on paper. It is striking that one of the episodes of the novel frequently takes up a whole page, from edge to edge. In order to fit it on one page Bernhard reduces the space between lines again and again from one and half spaces to one and writes to the very edge of the paper. This leads to the conclusion that Bernhard really carried his writing forward from page to page. The fact that the rhythmical structure produced was an important aspect for him may be assumed, not least, from his own statements as, for example, in *Drei Tage/Three Days*, where he describes his writing as a ›musical process‹ (I 147). And it is indeed amazing with what precision he writes the individual episodes in the space accorded.

The complete text is composed of numerous such ›page episodes‹ (some take up two pages exactly, or exactly three type-written pages) thus fulfilling a further criterion of mainly constructive writing. Hurlebusch sees such a method substantiated ›in the process of referring back to oneself in writing‹ (Hurlebusch 1998, 46), the author's view of what has been written puts ›thinking under the power and dynamics of the eye‹ (ibid., 43), and has decisive genetic importance for the continued writing of the text as well as its revision. The latter is itself manifested in a much later working phase in Bernhard's novel *Frost* in that he apparently kept changing the position of individual episodes within the novel until the very end. The fact that these individual elements are interchangeable is, beyond that, a significant advantage for the author – compared with his protagonists who always have the final text in mind – in that it leaves each written text as it was, in the ›mode of trial action‹ (ibid., 45) and in so doing covers up the recurring horror of vacuity on facing a sheet of white paper, it overcomes the ›difficulty of beginning‹ (I 149).

When the pressure of writing is relieved in this way it can, on the one hand, become, for the author, ›a means of fulfilment in raising oneself both aesthetically and mentally‹ (Hurlebusch 1998, 42) and on the other, a kind of ›jack‹ (ibid., 43) for thoughts, fragments of memory, pictures of the imagination, but also for the semi- and subconscious. When he is writing a psychogenetic function develops in

that the author, through the trial-action of writing, is able to solve biographical conflicts, for example, in a symbolic way. There are also sufficient indications of this in *Frost* whereby, naturally, the autobiographical elements in the novel deriving from his family history appear transformed and defamiliarized when divided up between the family history of the painter Strauch and the medical student. As early poems show, his coming to terms with his own biography and family history in his work does not just begin with the five volumes of autobiography, nor does it end there. On the contrary, Thomas Bernhard's writing represents an uninterrupted process of self-production which started early on and did not end until his death, a process in which the published works really only represent stages in a much longer path. In conclusion, to let Bernhard have his say once more: ›It is also wrong to really finish writing a so-called chapter of a book [...]. And the biggest mistake is when an author finishes writing a book.‹ (I 158)

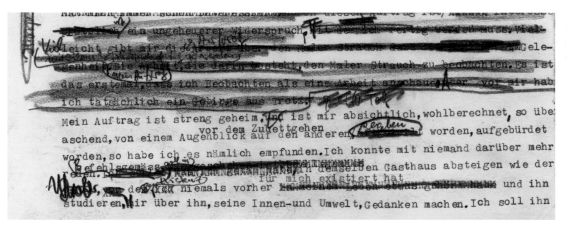

Frost, segment from the typed manuscript

In this essay we did not especially indicate which of Bernhard's texts have actually been translated into English. A list of these translated texts can be found in Bernhard's biography, p. 158f. The other titles are loose translations of the German originals.

Quotations from Bernhard's texts were taken from the following translations:

Cor   *Correction*, trans. Sophie Wilkens. New York: Knopf 1979.
GE   *Gathering Evidence. A Memoir*, trans. David McLintock. New York: Vintage 1993.

Otherwise the German versions of Bernhard´s texts were used and translated for this essay:

GG   *Gesammelte Gedichte*, ed. by Volker Bohn. Frankfurt am Main: Suhrkamp 1991.
 I   *Der Italiener*. Salzburg: Residenz 1971.

Further texts:

Dittmar, Jens (ed.): *Thomas Bernhard. Werkgeschichte*. Updated edition. Frankfurt am Main: Suhrkamp 1990
Hurlebusch, Klaus: *Den Autor besser verstehen: aus seiner Arbeitsweise. Prolegomenon zu einer Hermeneutik textgenetischen Schreibens*. In: *Textgenetische Edition*, ed by Hans Zeller and Gunter Martens. Tübingen: Niemeyer 1998 (= Beihefte zu Editio 10) pp. 7-51.
Plachta, Bodo: *Editionswissenschaft. Eine Einführung in Methode und Praxis der Edition neuerer Texte*. Stuttgart: Reclam 1997.

Thomas Bernhard,
Mayrwies 1951

Die Königin der
Städte

Du schönste Stadt am Salzachfluss,

Ich schloss dich in mein Herz,

Trotz täglich starkem Regenguss,

Und kindlich harten Schmerz.

Du Königin der Städte all,

Beherrbergst mich seit Jahren,

Auf diesem runden Erdenball,

In vielen Kedtgefahren.

Und sollt' Ich einmal nimmer sein,

So holt mich aus der Ferne

Und grabt mich in der Salzstadt ein,

D ort unterm Abendsterne.

.x.x.x.x.x.x.x.x.x.x.x.x.x.

Die Königin der Städte/The Queen of the Cities, typed manuscripts

Early example of Bernhard´s writings from 1948. The handwritten comments (›good‹) were probably
made by Johannes Freumbichler

Auf den schwarzen Truhen der Bauernerde
  steht geschrieben, daß ich sterben muß im Winter,
verlassen von meinen Sonnen und vom Geraune der
            Kübel,
  der vollgemolkenen,
Qual und Ende sprechend unter den Schlägen des
            Märzwinds,
  der mich vernichtet mit dem Gedanken
an die Apfelblüten und den Zauber der Tennen!
  Niemals habe ich eine Nacht zerstört mit
            Schimpfwörtern
und Tränen, aber diese Zeit, diese unsinnige Zeit,
  wird mich auslöschen
mit ihrer trockenen, messerscharfen Poesie!
  Ich werde nicht nur Verlassenheit erdulden müssen,
            sondern
das Vieh meiner Väter und Mütter durch die
            Jahrtausende treiben!
  Ich werde Regen erschaffen müssen
und Schnee und Mütterlichkeit
  für meine Verbrechen und den Zorn rühmen,
der mir das Getreide auf den eigenen Feldern ruiniert!
  Ich werde die Händler und Samstaghuren in einem
            Waldstück zusammenrufen,
und dieses Land, dieses traurige Land,
  ihrer wilden Verzweiflung schenken!
Ich werde tausend Sonnen hereinkommen lassen
            in meinen
  Hunger! Morgen werde ich

12

Vergängliche erschaffen für die Unsterblichkeit,
  nahe der Brunnen und Türme und fern
der Handwerker,
  in einer Frühe, die meiner Leiden überdrüssig ist
und in der nichts geschieht als der Heimgang der
            Sterne . . .
  . . . dort will ich mit den Verzweifelten sprechen
und alles zurücklassen,
  was Verachtung, Bitternis und Trauer war auf
            dieser Erde.

Auf der Erde und in der Hölle/
On Earth and in Hell,
Salzburg: Otto Müller 1957.
First volume of poetry

BRUCHSTÜCKE AUS EINER STERBENDEN STADT

I

Wenn ich müde bin, roll ich mein Hirn auf den Platz
und lasse die Füße trampeln und die Gemeinheit der
Metzger psalmieren.
Aus dem Loch eines Straßenbahnzuges schaue ich in den
Himmel,
vom Zittern der Blätter verwirrt und vom Lippen-
stülpen der Mädchen.
Ich flüchte in ein Milchgeschäft, wo sie traurig ihr
Frühstück trinken
und an die Sonne denken, die nicht mehr kommt.
In grauen Mänteln schlafen sie und ahnen den Tod
vieler grüner Hügel.

II

Ich höre die Stimmen der Vögel unter dem Himmel
und das Geplätscher des Baches.
Ich schleppe unser verlassenes Dorf herein
und lasse die Milch aus Millionen Eutern jubeln!
Ich werfe tausend Münzen in die Hochzeitskapelle,
die den besoffenen Bauern Ruhm bringt . . .

III

Die Lichter tönen wie rotes Fleisch in den Mitter-
nachtsgassen,
und doch ist meine Sprache die Sprache des Winds,
der über den Anger bläst wie am ältesten Tag,
der die Greuel der Wüsten bringt und die Sehnsucht
der trunkenen Palmbäume
nach dem Acker meines Vaters.

32

IV

Ich esse mein Brot auf einem Fensterplatz und
schaue in ihr Gesicht, das dem Fleisch der Löwen gleicht
und der Vernichtung.
Ich sehe ihr Hirn abtropfen auf den verkommenen
Teppich der Bauerndörfer,
die soviel Schmerz nie getrunken haben wie in diesen
Tagen,
da ich sie aufgab und von schwärzlichem Mitternachts-
honig lebe
hinter meinen flüssiggewordenen Augen.

V

Ich habe sie nicht gerufen, aber sie verfinstern meine
Stimme.
Doch jeder soll wissen, daß ich verlernt habe zu beten,
denn ich bin verkommen an einem Augusttag
des Jahres 1952,
jeder soll wissen, daß ich erstickt bin in meinem Fleisch.

VI

Niemand hört meine Stimme, die mich vernichten wird.
Sie werden mein Haus umzingeln und meine Tür
eintreten und den Namen rufen,
auf den ich höre.
Sie werden vergessen, daß auch ich der Schöpfer
des Grases
und der Erhalter der Milch und des Honigs bin.
In einem Winkel der Traurigkeit werden sie mich
erschlagen,
wenn Schnee und Wind und Frühling zu spät kommen...

3

33

First edition of Bernhards first volume of poetry with corrections

4

DER SELBSTMÖRDER ~~geht~~ in den Wald ~~um sich zurückzuziehen~~. Er benützt
den Hohlweg. Dort entdeckt er, dass er ~~zeit seines Lebens~~ nicht genug
Wärme gehabt hat. Diese Feststellung entwickelt sich in seinem Gehirn
zu einem ungeheueren Schmerz, ~~der Dimensionen annimmt~~, denen er ratlos
gegenüber steht. ~~Er begreift~~ plötzlich nicht, warum er mit seinem Ent-
schluss so lange gewartet hat. ~~Er stülpt seine Hosentaschen um und~~ richtet den Blick auf einen Gegenstand, ~~von dem er nicht weiss, wie er ihn
benennen soll. Deshalb zieht er sich von ihm zurück.~~ Er lässt den Gegenstand, ein Tier, oder einen Menschen, liegen, als wollte er sagen, es habe
keinen Sinn, sich in eine noch viel gefährlichere Situation zu begeben.
~~Aber diese Überlegungen helfen ihm nicht.~~ Er setzt seinen Weg fort, folge-
richtig, ohne Umschweife. ~~Ohne Überlegungen gleich welcher Natur.~~ Er er-
greift die Gelegenheit, in der Finsternis unterzutauchen. Gewaltsam läuft
er in die Finsternis hinein. Die paar Augenblicke, die ihm wie eine dump-
fe stille Wasseroberfläche den Hals ~~XXXXXXXXXX~~ durchschneiden, zerstört er blitz-
artig, indem er sich in den Strick fallen lässt, der ihm, fast lautlos,
das Genick bricht.

LCB-Editionen

Ereignisse

Thomas Bernhard

*Der Selbstmörder/The Suicide Victim,
Der Hauptmann/The Captain*, typed copy from
Ereignisse/Incidents

Ereignisse/Incidents,
Berlin: Literarisches Colloquium 1969

Ereignisse/Incidents – completed in 1957 – was
to have been printed by the S. Fischer publishing
company. Bernhard decided not to publish it

DER HAUPTMANN ist in die Bezirksstadt abkommandiert, strafweise,
~~aber diese Versetzung ist ihm willkommen, ja, es ist ihm, als hätte~~
~~er schon jahrelang von dieser Versetzung geträumt, obwohl er nicht~~
~~einen Menschen in der Bezirksstadt kennt. Aber vielleicht gerade~~
~~deshalb, er hat bisher noch nicht einmal von der Existenz dieses~~
~~Ortes gehört, nicht, weil er beschränkter ist, als andere Hauptleute,~~
~~die alle beschränkt sind, sondern weil er sich niemals für die Geo-~~
~~graphie seines Landes interessiert hat. Und über sein Land hinaus~~
~~ist er geistig niemals gedrungen.~~ Es ist ein kalter Morgen, ~~es ist~~
neblig, niemand würde, müsste er nicht, ~~wäre er nicht gezwungen,~~ aufsteh-
en. Aber der Hauptmann kommandiert seine Mannschaft in den Kasernenhof,
schreit, ~~dass sie ihm am liebsten empörigen würden, aber~~ die beiden
Unteroffiziere, zwanzigjährige ~~Burschen vom Land,~~ hat er so gut in der
Hand, dass sie in Minutenschnelle die Männer aufgestellt haben. ~~In~~
~~Reihe.~~ Der Hauptmann ruft ein paar Namen, dann tritt er vor ~~das~~
~~Formation~~ und befiehlt den Unteroffizieren, ~~den angetretenen Män-~~
~~nern~~ die Köpfe abzuschneiden, der Reihe nach. Da sein Befehl ~~wie seine~~
~~vorangegangenen Befehle ausgedrückt~~ ist, beginnen die beiden Unteroffiziere widerspruchslos mit dem Abschneiden der Köpfe ihrer Unter-
gebenen. Diese getrauen sich nichts zu erwidern und sind schliesslich
alle geköpft, bleiben aber, da sie keinen anderen Befehl ~~bekommen~~ haben,
~~stram~~ stehen. Als das der Hauptmann, ~~der fühlt die Unteroffiziere~~
~~die Köpfe abschnitten, bemerkt, er habe an etwas ganz anderes~~
~~gedacht, bemerkt,~~ bricht er in ein nicht endenwollendes Gelächter aus,
das auch dann noch zu hören ist, als man ihn und die beiden Unteroffiziere in einem verschlossenen Wagen in die Irrenanstalt ~~Stadt~~ abtransportiert.

Marginal handwritten notes: 4 Es · 4 Burschen · erstarrte Glied · un umstöss... · bewegungslos · schwimmt

Bottom handwritten note: Minutenschnelle ?

Thomas Bernhard,
St. Veit im Pongau
1956

*Eine Maschine/
A Machine*,
typed manuscript

EINE MASCHINE,die wie eine Guillotine konstruiert ist,schneidet von
einer sich langsam fortbewegenden Gummimasse grosse Stücke ab und
lässt sie auf ein Fliessband fallen,das sich einen Stock tiefer fort-
bewegt und an welchem Hilfsarbeiterinnen sitzen,die die abgeschnittener
Stücke zu kontrollieren und schliesslich in grosse Kartons zu verpacker
haben.Die Maschine ist erst neun Wochen in Betrieb genommen und der
Tag,an welchem sie der ~~xxxxxxxxx~~ Fabriksleitung übergeben wurde,
wird niemand,der bei dieser Feierlichkeit anwesend war,vergessen.Sie
ist auf einem eigens für sie konstruierten Eisenbahnwaggon in die Fabrik geschafft worden und die Festredner haben betont,dass die Maschine eine der grössten Errungenschaften der Technik darstelle.Sie ist
bei ihrem Eintreffen in der Fabrik von einer Musikkapelle begrüsst worden und die Arbeiter und die Ingenieure ~~haben~~ sie mit abgenommenen
~~Hüten~~ ~~empfangen~~ Ihre Montage ~~dauerte~~ vierzehn Tage und die Besitzer ~~konnten~~ sich
von ihrer Arbeitsleistung und Zuverlässigkeit überzeugen.Sie muss nur
regelmässig,und zwar alle vierzehn Tage,mit besonderen Ölen geschmiert
werden.Zu diesem Zweck muss eine Arbeiterin eine Stahlwendeltreppe er-
klettern und das Öl durch ein Ventil langsam einfliessen lassen.Der
Arbeiterin ~~wird~~ wurde alles bis ins Kleinste erklärt.Trotzdem rutscht das
Mädchen ~~neun Wochen nach der Montage~~ so unglücklich aus,dass es geköpft wird.Sein Kopf platzt wie die Gummistücke hinunter.Die Arbeiterinnen,die am Fliessband sitzen,sind ~~jedoch~~ so entsetzt,dass keine von
ihnen schreien kann.Sie behandeln den Mädchenkopf gewohnheitsmässig
wie die Gummistücke.Die Letzte nimmt den Kopf und verpackt ihn in einem Karton.

Thomas Bernhard
at the Mozarteum in
Salzburg, 1956

Der Schauspieler/
The Actor,
typed manuscript

H spielt.

DER SCHAUSPIELER tritt in einem Märchenspiel auf ~~das einer seiner Freunde für ihn geschrieben hat und in dem~~ er die Rolle ~~des~~ bösen Zauberers ~~zu spielen hat, zu welchem Zweck~~ *Er wird* er in einen Schafspelz gesteckt ~~wird und auch noch~~ in ein Paar viel zu kurze Schuhe, die ihm die Füsse zusammen pressen. Das ganze Gewand ist so unangenehm, dass er in Schweiss ausbricht, aber das sieht ja niemand und überhaupt spielt er vor ~~niemand~~ *keinem* so gern ~~als~~ *wie* vor Kindern, denn sie sind das dankbarste Publikum ~~das er sich vorstellen kann und das er tatsächlich kennt, oder zumindest zu kennen glaubt~~. Die Kinder, dreihundert ~~an der Zahl~~, erschrecken bei seinem Auftritt, denn sie sind ganz für das junge Paar eingenommen, das ~~er Zauberer~~ in zwei ungleiche Tiere ~~sie~~ verzaubert. ~~Und sie~~ Am liebsten würden sie nur das junge, in bunte Kleider gehüllte Paar sehen, ~~und~~ sonst nichts, aber dann wäre das Spiel kein gutes Spiel und schon nach kurzer Zeit langweilig; denn zu einem richtigen Märchenspiel gehört seit jeher eine bösartige, undurchschaubare Gestalt, die das Gute, Durchschaubare, zu zerstören oder wenigstens lächerlich zu machen trachtet. Da nun zum zweitenmal der Vorhang aufgeht, sind die Kinder nicht mehr zu halten. Sie stürzen aus den Sesseln und auf die Bühne und es ist, als wären es nicht mehr nur dreihundert, sondern ein Vielfaches dieser Zahl und obwohl der Schauspieler unter der Maske weint und sie anfleht, doch einzuhalten mit ihren Fusstritten und Schlägen, die sie ihm mit harten, metallenen Gegenständen versetzen, lassen sie sich nicht beeinflussen und schlagen solange auf ihn ein und trampeln solange auf ihm herum, bis er sich nicht mehr rührt und seine bleichen verstümmelten Hände in die staubige Luft des Schnürbodens hinein ragen. Als die anderen Schauspieler herbeigeeilt kommen und feststellen, dass ihr Mitspieler tot ist, brechen die Kinder in ein ungeheueres Gelächter aus, das so gross ist, dass sie darin alle den Verstand verlieren.

Flüchten

+ besteigen

ZWEI JUNGE LEUTE betreten einen ~~alten~~ Turm, der zur Verteidigung der
Stadt ~~in den Jahren 1154 und 1156~~ diente und ~~beschliessen,~~ ihn zu
~~besteigen,~~ ohne ein Wort zu sprechen. Sie wollen ihr Schweigen nicht
durch einen Verrat auslöschen und gehen mit gedankenloser Schnellig-
keit an ihr Vorhaben. In halber Höhe des Turms erblicken sie einen
nicht errechenbaren Ausschnitt der Landschaft, in welcher der Turm
steht. Die Kälte der Mauern lässt sie wie in einem Eisklumpen zur
Höhe taumeln. Mit offenen Mündern und nach vorwärts ausgestreckten
Armen, in der Idee, dass sie durch diese halbwahren Gebärden die Ent-
fernung, die sie zurücklegen wollen, künstlich verringern können. Nun
zeigt sich, dass das Mädchen durch ihre Phantasie grössere Schnellig-
keit betreiben kann als der geistig beschränkte junge Mann und es ist
wichtig, festzustellen, dass das Mädchen, obwohl es acht oder zehn
Treppen hinter dem jungen Mann, ihrem Liebhaber, emporsteigt, in Wahrheit ihm um fünfzehn oder zwanzig Treppenlängen voraus ist. Der ~~ers~~
~~auf das~~ völlig fensterlose Turm ist eine Vorstufe der Finsternis und
als solche ganz deutlich erkennbar. ~~Dann aber~~ ~~die in Wirklichkeit~~ Als sie endlich oben angekommen sind, ziehen sie sich aus und fallen sich nackt in die Arme.

Lm

Lte

(Verb)

völlig

besser
als alt

alt 10 .   (An den Anfang)

Zwei junge Leute/
Two Young People,
typed manuscript

Thomas Bernhard
at the North Sea 1956

Thomas Bernhard, Maja and Gerhard Lampersberg, late 1950s

*Gartenspiel für den Besitzer eines Lusthauses in Kärnten/
Garden Play for the Owner of a House of Pleasure in Carinthia*,
typed manuscript of an unpublished short drama from Bernhard´s
time at the Tonhof/Carinthia (1957-1960)

GARTENSPIEL
FÜR
DEN
~~EINEN MOND LÄNGER~~
BESITZER
EINES
LUSTHAUSES
IN
KÄRNTEN

> Auf mein Wort,Nerissa,meine kleine
> Person ist dieser grossen Welt
> überdrüssig...
>
> Shakespeare,Kaufmann von Venedig

Im Garten vor dem Lusthaus.Ein Frühlingsabend.Die Dunkelheit kommt
über die Szenerie.Die SCHAUSPIELERIN,als wäre sie von einer grös-
seren,anstrengenden Reise zurückgekehrt,

> leise
>> Der Sommer,der Herbst,
>> der Winter...
>> Ich war überall.
>> Überall.
>> Ich bezahl nichts,worüber
>> ich lache.
>> Oh...

LANDMÄDCHEN

> lacht und tritt auf

Thomas Bernhard at the Mozarteum in Salzburg around 1956

Eine intelligente Tote/An Intelligent Dead Woman (*Frühling/Spring*), typed manuscript

Frühling/Spring premiered in 1960 at the ›Theater am Tonhof‹ along with *Die Erfundene/ The Invented One*, *Rosa/Rose*, and the short opera, *Köpfe/Heads*, composed by Gerhard Lampersberg, directed by Herbert Wochinz

~~FRÜHLING~~ [Eine intelligente Tote]

Die Sängerin
Der Arzt
Das Stubenmädchen
Die Hausfrau
Zwei Leichenträger

(Aufgeräumtes Zimmer)

Sängerin: (auf dem Totenbett)
                   In früheren Jahren
                   ~~erkannte ich mich in jedem~~ Spiegel
                   ~~als die, die ich immer gewesen bin.~~
                   Später fuhr ich aufs Land
                   und kostete von den Äpfeln,
                   ~~die ich seit meiner Kindheit~~
                   ~~nicht mehr genossen habe.~~
                   ~~Ich beurteile die Früchte~~
                   ~~nach dem Reichtum ihres Geruchs.~~
                   ~~Allmählich werden sie süsser~~
                   ~~und ich sterblicher~~
                   ~~und ein dumpfer Glockenschlag sagt mir,~~
                   ~~dass alles keinen Sinn hat~~
                   ~~ohne die Süssigkeit,~~
                   ~~die mich älter werden lässt.~~

Arzt: Worüber denken Sie nach?

Sängerin: An eine Arie und an den Ton,
                   den ich niemals erreichen konnte.
                   ~~Ich wollte ihn erreichen.~~
                   ~~Ich entblösste mich in dieser Musik.~~
                   ~~Aber~~ ich vollzog das alles,
                   ohne die Aufmerksamkeit der Welt
                   auf mich zu ziehen.

Arzt: ~~Haben Sie sich nie an den Verfall gewöhnt,~~
                   ~~der in den Zweigen beginnt~~
                   ~~und sich über Erdteile ausbreitet?~~

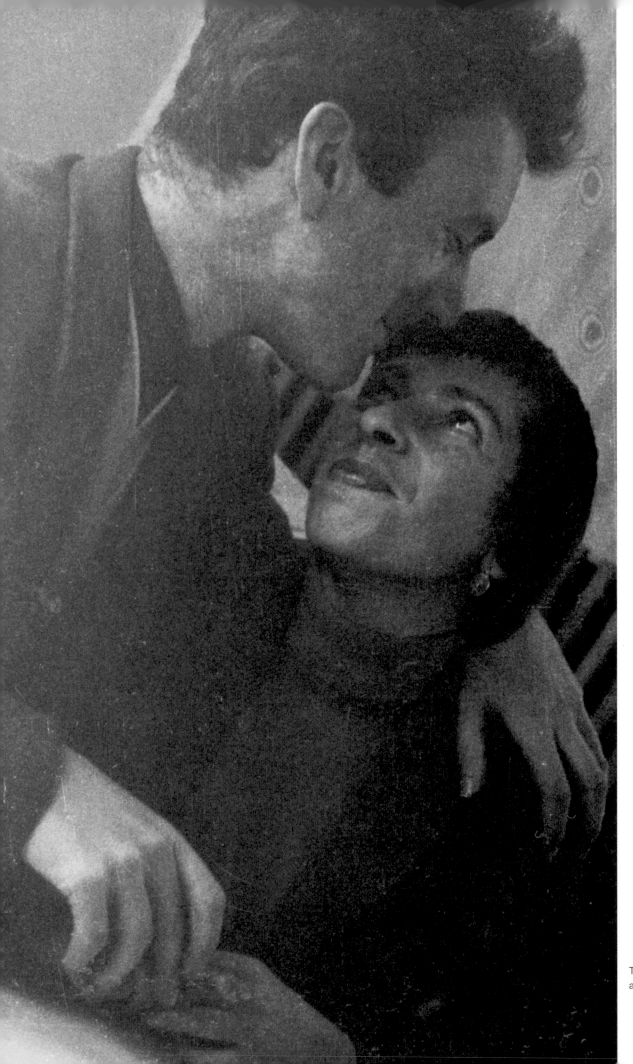

Thomas Bernhard
and Jeannie Ebner

er geht voraus durch das Dickicht, versucht, das Gestrüpp auseinander
zu halten, aber das macht er so ungeschickt, dass das Fräulein jetzt
schon ganz zerkratzt ist,
ich gehe lieber voraus, sagt sie und zieht mit ihrer Rechten an seinem
Rockärmel, ganz plötzlich und so, dass er erschrocken ist,
wie sie aus dem Jungwald herausläuft und unter den Fichtenstämmen
durch, hat er Mühe, ihr nachzukommen, die furchtbare Nacht, die er hinter sich hat, steckt noch in seinen Gliedern, er schwitzt, aber er will
sie nicht aus den Augen lassen, die Bucklich,
jetzt ist sie im Hohlweg untergetaucht, um bald auf der anderen Seite
wieder herauszukommen,
er bemüht sich, stolpert aber und fällt mit dem Gesicht voraus in den
Hohlweg hinein, ja, es nützt nichts, ich muss aufstehen, die Hose hat
einen Riss, das nackte Knie schaut heraus, er hat es sich abgeschürft,
ist mit der Sandale hängen geblieben, das Fräulein hat nichts davon
bemerkt, sie läuft immer weiter, <u>ihr nach</u> !, sie läuft im Zickzack, einmal taucht sie auf der linken, dann wieder auf der rechten Seite auf,
immer kleiner,

Der Wald auf der Straße/The Forest on the Street, typed manuscript

Early attempt at writing novels before *Frost*
with a later handwritten critique

THOMAS BERNHARD

DER WALD AUF DER STRASSE
ROMAN

der roman !
Mist !
wie kann was
passieren ?
Aufgeblasenes Nix !
ja, ja, Mist !!

Thomas Bernhard and (behind him) Wieland Schmied, Maria Saal (Corinthia)

Tamsweg, typed manuscript

Bernhard tried to convince various publishers to publish the text
which was written in 1960, but no one accepted the manuscript.
In several aspects *Tamsweg* prefigures his novel, *Frost*

der Tod im Wald, der Tod hinter der ~~Aufbahrungskammer, den Tod, der~~
~~den~~ Schnee ~~~~, der Tod, der in den Schulkindern ist; der Tod
ist ein Geruch, kein Geräusch, der Tod ist der erste Geruch, ~~das Auf-~~
~~nehmen der Seele in uns ist das Einatmen des ersten Todesgeruchs.~~

Im Grunde existieren für ~~uns~~ nur die Menschen, die uns wenigstens
einmal gequält haben, die anderen, die ~~keine Qual in uns zustande ge-~~
~~bracht haben, haben~~ für uns nie gelebt; die Erinnerung an diese Un-
glücklichen hört eines Tages auf und war schon lange vorher lächerlich; es gibt keinen Menschen, den ich jemals geliebt habe und der
mich nicht ein einziges Mal gequält hätte; je eindringlicher die
Qualen, die uns von einem Menschen zugefügt werden, desto eindringlicher die Liebe, die wir für diesen Menschen empfinden; das Zusam-
mensein mit meiner Mutter war nichts anderes als unausgesetzte
~~bis ins allerkleinste, ja bis in unsichtbare Einzelheiten hinein,~~
~~vorausberechnete Qual, meinen Vater habe ich nie gesehen, Also war~~
~~ich die Qual, die ich durch ihn erlitten habe noch hundertmal grösser;~~
~~meine Halbgeschwister schliesslich haben die Kraft solcher Qualen~~
~~und Qualerei nicht mehr aufgebracht; vielleicht gibt es noch zwei,~~
~~drei Menschen, die eine solche Qual für mich erzeugt haben, aber ich~~
meine ~~natürlich~~ nicht die gewöhnliche Qual.

Alles, was du ~~anschaust~~, wartet darauf, erlöst zu werden; aber wer
wird es erlösen ?, wer ~~erlösen können~~ ?, einzig und allein der Tod;
und diesen Tod soll man fürchten ?, niemand fürchtet den Tod, aber
er will nicht zugeben, den Tod als höchstes zukünftiges Ereignis
vor allen anderen Erscheinungen zu lieben; ja mehr zu lieben als
alles, was uns die Religion und die Natur gelehrt haben; wer den Tod
~~vor sich~~ hat, braucht nicht ~~niemals~~ zu fürchten; die reinste Liebe
ist die Liebe für den Tod; das höchste Glück ist, diese Liebe zu
erreichen.

Der Schatten des Einzelgängers, ~~der einem~~ die Geschwindigkeit, ~~die~~
~~~~ Gestalt ~~zurücklegt~~, mitteilt, ~~und dann auch~~ sein Gesicht ~~und~~
~~seinen ganzen~~ Körper; ~~es ist halb fünf~~ Uhr, er geht ~~ins Armenhaus;~~
die Gedanken, ~~die er hat, sind auch deine Gedanken, die alle~~ Menschen-

Thomas Bernhard and Rudolf Brändle (left) with some of their acquaintances, Goldegg 1950

Schwarzach St. Veit, typed manuscript

Fair copy of the completed novel
with date on the title page

THOMAS BERNHARD

SCHWARZACH SANKT VEIT

ROMAN

ERSTES KAPITEL

Immer läuft er zwischen den Gräbern herum, ~~herumzulaufen~~ *geht* da und dort hin,
liest den und den Namen,lange Namen,kurze Namen,völlig bedeutungslose
Namen,geht erst wieder nach Hause,wenn ihn fröstelt,wenn er Hunger hat,
und todmüde ist,das Fräulein ist mit ihrer Grossmutter immer schon auf
die Friedhöfe gegangen,kaum hat sie gehen können,hat ihre Grossmutter
sie auf die Friedhöfe geschleppt,in die Aufbahrungshallen hinein,wenn
man sich abschliesst,wenn man nicht ab und zu alle paar Tage,alle paar
Wochen wenigstens Menschen aufsucht oder zu sich in das Zimmer herein-
lässt,denkt David,kann man es überhaupt nicht mehr aushalten,immer wieder
muss man sich an irgendeinen Menschen heranmachen,versuchen,einen dieser
rätselhaften fremden Menschen,die wir gut kennen und die uns doch das ganze Leben lang fremd bleiben und rätselhaft,deren Namen wir aus der früh-
esten Kindheit kennen und die nichts über uns wissen und über die wir
nichts wissen,nichts wissen wir,als ihren Namen und den vergessen wir
immer wieder,immer wieder braucht man einen Menschen,in entscheidenen
Tagen und in weniger wichtigen,aber wir brauchen einen,den wir auf unsere Leiden aufmerksam machen können,auf unseren Hunger und auf unsere
fortwährenden Phantasien und auf unseren Unsinn,auf unsere Fehler und auf
unser Absterben,das begonnen hat,als wir auf die Welt gekommen sind und
das von Tag zu Tag deutlicher wird und schliesslich sehen wir überhaupt
nichts mehr als unser Absterben,es hat keinen Sinn,sich gegen dieses
Absterben zu wehren,es zu verleugnen,ihm ins Gesicht zu schauen,es nützt
nichts,umso furchtbarer ist es,man muss etwas tun,dann ist *es* verträglich,
Handgriffe,nichts als Handgriffe,irgendwelche Tätigkeiten des Körpers
und des Geistes,sonst/sind wir die restlichen Jahre tot und waren immer
tot und müssen fortwährend und immer unseren eigenen Tod anschauen und
das würde uns wahnsinnig machen,du bist,denkt David,ein grosser Schriftsteller,du bist Catull und Dante und Shakespeare zugleich und der
Schwarm grosser Dichter nach ihnen,du bist der einzige und letzte und
erste und der grösste in deinem Zustand und redest in deinem Zustand
mit ihren Wörtern in die furchtbare Stille hinein,in das Wälderrauschen,
in das Städterauschen,redest und redest und kannst nicht mehr aufhören
und kannst nicht mehr zurück und niemand hört dich und alle hören dich
und niemand,Labil hat jetzt wieder das bestimmte Gefühl,bald sterben zu
müssen,woher dieses Gefühl kommt,weiss er nicht,plötzlich ist es da,wie
schön doch dieser Friedhof angelegt ist,sagt das Fräulein,sie habe sich
schon oft gedacht,wenn sie stürbe,wolle sie hier begraben sein,wenn sie
stürbe,aber wer wird mich hierher bringen ?,sagt sie,sie hat Gedanken,
wie man sie in ihrem Alter nicht mehr hat,sie hat richtige Todesgedanken,

denkt

oben im Dorf das Begräbnis,die Leute,die einen Kreis um die Kirche herum
und ihre Gedanken dahertragen wie Prangerstangen,die lautlose
Einbalsamierung des Nachmittags,die stupide Ruhe, mit der das
Tal angefüllt ist,der Regen,der hinter dem Kitzsteinhorn niedergegangen
ist...die schwarzen Schützen, die Gebetbücher im
Gras,der Pfarrer staaft sich fortwährend Lügen,aber was er sagt,ist gut,
weil es einfach ist...die Wirtsfrau mit ihrem Verachtung gegen jeden Hungri-
gen,und jedem Durstigen,der Tischler mit seinem Übelwollen gegen die Schul-
kinder,der Lehrer mit seinem kleinen Verstand,mit seiner Trägheit,mit
seiner Homosexualität,der Doktor mit seinem Holzbein,ein Opfer des Zweiten Weltkriegs,seine Tochter Geschirrspülerin in einem Gasteiner Hotel,
die Mutter von sieben blödsinnigen Kindern,die als Letzte daherkommt,weiss
nicht,wie sie dazukommt,Witwe zu sein und eben diese sieben blödsinnigen
Kinder zu haben...das Dorf sauft vier Prozent des Schnapses jährlich,den
man für das ganze Land berechnet hat...darum die Kleinheit,die Blödheit,
aber der wunderbare Instinkt für das Absterben,für den Kot...das Zibo-
rium,das Sanktus,das Angus Dei,die Trompetenstösse,die Orgel,die über
alles weht wie ein Herbststurm,alle Lügen,alle Wetter zerstört,klaren Himmel schafft...das reine Gedächtnis der Organistin,die Blösse,die sie sich
gibt,aber der wunderbare Ausdruck ihres Gesichts,ihre
Erbarmungslosigkeit gegenüber dem Nächsten,gegenüber jedem Gefallenen,
ihre blinde Anhängerschaft im Zeichen Christi...der Bäcker mit seinem Glatzkopf,
immer der Erste,mit ein paar Brocken Latein sichert er sich die Position
neben dem Pfarrer,hat den Doktor mit dem Holzbein verdrängt,schaut nurmehr
noch herunter...die Fabriksarbeiterin (Fünftagewoche in der Schokoladenfa-
brik Schatzmann in Schwarzach!) versucht nicht einmal,die Augen im geeig-
neten Moment zu schliessen,ihre Einfältigkeit hat sie vor den ewigen Richter berufen...und dieses ewige EWIG,EWIG,EWIG,das so stupid
ist und alle vom richtigen Weg abbringt,selbst der Pfarrer
eingefallen ist,aber er ist nicht der einzige,die ganze Kirche ist diesem
ewigen EWIG,EWIG,EWIG...(der Opfertod des
Weltanschauung)
wenn der Regen da ist,rühren sie sich nicht vom Fleck,aber er wird nicht
kommen,bevor sie den Friedhof verlassen haben...strenge Gesichter,nicht so
unnachgebig wie die im Flachgau...Scheinheilig-
keit vermischt mit Föhnangst...oft nichts als eine reine Gebährmutternspie-
lerei...die Rosenkärnze im Schla
alles im Schlaf...das Wort Gottes wie das Wort Brot als reine Widerwärtig-
keit...dazu der tägliche Umgang mit minderwertigen Kühen,mit trich-
ninverseuchten Schweinen,die vor meinem ebenerdigen Fenster einen ent-
setzlichen kaum hörbaren Lärm machen...

WEISST DU

Weisst Du,
der Sommer stirbt in Deinem Schlaf,
kümmert sich nicht um Deine Vorbereitungen,
ist nicht auf Deiner Hochzeit,

kommt nicht zu den Toten hinunter,

redet nicht von Schweigen und Früchteschwängern.

Weisst Du,
die Nacht stirbt in Deinem Schlaf,
wendet sich ab von Dir,Unsinnige,
fährt über Deinen Rücken,
zerquetscht Äpfel und Birnen,tötet
in ihrem Schleim Deine Tempel,

Weisst Du
mit Deinem Sterben beschicke ich
ihre Märkte,rede den Bauern ein,
Du wärst in dieser Kuh gefangen und rührstest Dich nicht
für alle ihre unausgeschlafenen Seelen,

flögst heimlich auf mit den Vögeln über ihre Dächer.

Schwarzach St. Veit, typed manuscript of an early version, 1957. Notes on the back from an earlier typed manuscript of poetry

FROST
~~MICH FRIERT~~

Mich friert,
der Winter an der Böschung zieht mir
die Gelenke zusammen,den ganzen Jammer
   meiner ~~vertrunkenen~~ Jahre...
      Zerschundenen

mich friert,
vertrottelter Baum,zerschlissene Lüge
meiner Schmerzen,der Täler Geschrei
   aus den Leichentuchfetzen...

Mich friert,
hinunter muss ich und ewige Erde
mit nackten Knochen aufreissen auf dem Land,
ihr untertäniges Werk verrichten,
   zurücklassen meine Liebe.

Frost, typed manuscript of an unpublished volume of poetry

In 1961 Bernhard couldn't find a publisher for his volume
of poetry, entitled *Frost*

THOMAS BERNHARD

FROST

GEDICHTE

Thomas Bernhard with Christine Lavant and Hilde Spiel in the Gardens of Mirabell Palace, Salzburg, late 1950s

```
Auftrag

    I   Einleitung

   II   Ankunft, Umwelt des Gasthauses

        siebenmal Brief an Assistent
        und Meditation über den Maler Strauch mit
bis  IX Beobachtung

  X(XI?) sogenannter Abschiedsbrief des Malers an se
        inen Bruder (und Schwester ?)
   XI
  XII   dann sogenannte SÄTZE DES MALERS STRAUCH,
        die ich mir im Laufe der Tage im Gedächtnis
        und auf dem Papier notiert habein der

        Reihenfolge ihres Entstehens, nicht ihrer

        Bedeutung.
```

Draft of the novel *Frost* (shown here with the title *Auftrag/Mission*)

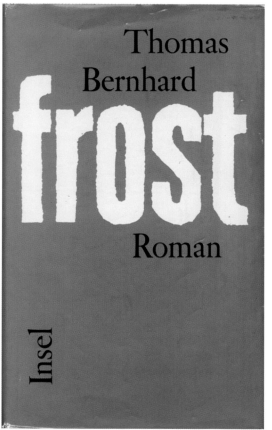

Frost,
Frankfurt am Main: Insel 1963

Bernhard´s novel *Frost* is his
first public literary success.

Thomas Bernhard, 1960s

On the following pages: Two versions of the beginning and ending of the novel

tur nes

... eine Famula
tur ... nicht nur ... Zuschauen bei komplizierten Darmoperationen,
Bauchfell aufschneiden, zuklammern und Fussabsägen, sie besteht
wirklich nicht/aus nur Totenaugenzudrücken und aus Kinderherausziehen in
die Welt; eine Famulatur ist nicht nur das: abgeschnittene ganze Beine und
Arme über die Schulter in den grossen Emailkübel werfen,
das ist sie nicht, auch besteht sie nicht aus dem ständig hinter dem Primarius und dem Assistenten und dem Assistenten des Assistenten dahertrotteln,
aus dem Schwanzdasein der Visite, nein daraus besteht ja eigentlich nicht
die Famulatur, nicht nur aus dem besteht sie, nicht nur aus Brustabwaschen
und ... aus Magenauspumpen und Herztöne abreissen,
aus dem Vorspiegeln falscher Tatsachen, nicht aus dem, dass ich
sage,"der Eiter wird sich ganz einfach in Ihrem Blut auflösen und dann sind
Sie gesund"und aus hunderterlei anderen Lügen, nicht nur daraus besteht ein-
e Famulatur, dass ich sage, das ist eine Ansammlung von Tuberkeln, wie
ich noch keine gesehen habe, und: das ist ein ganz schönes Krebsgeschwür,
das dem Assistenten zum rechten Zeitpunkt, nämlich zu seiner wichtigen Arbei
über die Krebsgeschwüre in der Gebärmutter, kommt ja. Eine Famulatur
nicht nur eine Lehrstelle für Aufschneiden und Zuschneiden,
Abbinden und Aushalten. Eine Famulatur muss auch mit ausserfleischlichen
und Möglichkeiten sich an den Famulanten heranarbeiten. Und vielleicht ist
mein Auftrag, nämlich, den Maler Strauch zu beobachten, eine solche ausserfleischliche
Tatsache, eine ausserfleischliche Möglichkeit. Und es kann ja sein, dass das, was
ausserfleischlich ist, ich meine damit nicht die Seele, von der ich
nicht weiss, ob es sie gibt, von der ich aber erwarte, dass es sie gibt, und es
sind viele Anzeichen für diese Annahme, für diese jahrtausendealte Vermutung
da, es kann also durchaus sein, dass das Ausserfleisch-
liche, nämlich das ohne/Zellen, das ist, worauf alles die existiert und nicht umgekehrt. Weil ich das nicht genau weiss, darum interessiert es mich. Mein
Durch diesen Auftrag ist/ Interesse
ein ungeheuerer Widerspruch ...
Vielleicht gibt mir die Arbeit über den Maler Strauch ... Gelegenheit. Die Arbeit, die darin besteht, den Maler Strauch zu beobachten. Es ist
das erstemal, dass ich Beobachten als eine Arbeit anschaue. Aber vor mir hab
ich tatsächlich ein Gebirge aus Trotz.

Mein Auftrag ist streng geheim. Und ist mir absichtlich, wohlberechnet, so über-
aschend, von einem Augenblick auf den anderen, vor dem Zubettgehen worden, aufgebürdet
worden, so habe ich es nämlich empfunden. Ich konnte mit niemand darüber mehr
reden. Befehlsgemäss in demselben Gasthaus absteigen wie der
für mich existiert hat
..., der niemals vorher ... und ihn
studieren, mir über ihn, seine Innen-und Umwelt, Gedanken machen. Ich soll ihn

Erster Tag

Eine Famulatur bestehtja nicht nur aus dem Zuschauen bei komplizierten
Darmoperationen, aus Bauchfellaufschneiden, Lungenflügelzuklammern und
Fussabsägen, sie besteht wirklich nicht nur aus Totenaugeneindrücken
und aus Kinderherausziehen in die Welt. Eine Famulatur ist nicht nur
das: abgesägte ganze und halbe Beine und Arme über die Schulter in
den Emailabfallkübel hineinwerfen. Auch besteht sie nicht aus dem ständig hinter dem Primarius und dem Assistenten und dem Assistenten des
Assistenten Dahertrotteln, aus dem Schwanzdasein der Visite. Aus dem
Vorspiegeln falscher Tatsachen allein kann eine Famulatur nicht bestehen, nicht aus dem, dass ich sage: "Der Eiter wird sich ganz einfach
in Ihrem Blut auflösen und Sie sind wieder gesund." Und aus hunderterlei anderen Lügen. Nicht nur daraus, dass ich sage: "Es wird schon!" - wo
nichts mehr wird. Eine Famulatur ist ja nicht nur eine Lehrstelle für
Aufschneiden und Zunähen, für Abbinden und Aushalten. Eine Famulatur
muss auch mit ausserfleischlichen Tatsachen und Möglichkeiten rechnen.
Mein Auftrag, nämlich den Maler Strauch zu beobachten, zwingt mich, mich
mit solchen ausserfleischlichen Tatsachen und Möglichkeiten auseinan-
derzusetzen. Etwas Unerforschliches zu erforschen. Es bis zu einem gewissen erstaunlichen Grad von Möglichkeiten aufzudecken. Wie man eine
Verschwörung aufdeckt. Und es kann ja sein, dass das Ausserfleischliche,
ich meine damit nicht die Seele, dass das, was ausserfleischlich ist, ohne
die Seele zu sein, von der ich ja nicht weiss, ob es sie gibt, von der
ich aber erwarte, dass es sie gibt, dass diese/Vermutung jahrtausendealte Wahrheit ist; es kann durchaus sein, dass das Ausserfleischliche,
nämlich das ohne die Zellen, das ist, worauf alles existiert und nicht
umgekehrt, und nicht nur eines auf dem andern.

Zweiter Tag

Ich bin mit dem ersten Zug gefahren, mit dem Halbfünfuhrzug. Durch Fels-
wände. Links und rechts war es schwarz. Mich fröstelte, als ich einstieg.
Dann wurde mir langsam warm. Zum Ersticken. Dazu die Stimmen von aus der
Nachtschicht heimkehrenden Arbeitern und Arbeiterinnen, denen sofort
meine Sympathie gilt. Einer entscheidenden Welt. Frauen und Männer, jung
und alt, aber gleichgestimmt, vom Kopf bis über die Brüste und über die
Hoden bis zu den Füssen übernächtig. Die Männer mit grauen Kappen, die
Frauen mit roten Kopftüchern. Ihre Beine haben sie in Lodenfetzen ein-
gewickelt, das ist die einzige Möglichkeit, der Kälte einen Strich durch
die Rechnung zu machen. Ich wusste gleich, dass es sich um eine Schnee-

Der Maler Strauch hat sich erschossen.Ich fahre sofort ▆▆▆ Schwarzach
zurück.Hoffentlich lassen sie mich in Ruhe.

Neun Tage nach meiner Rückkehr nach Schwarzach fand ich im "Salzburger
Volksblatt" folgende Notiz:"Der Berufslose G.Strauch aus Wien ist seit
Donnerstag vergangener Woche im Gemeindegebiet von Weng abgängig.Wegen
der herrschenden Schneefälle musste die Suchaktion nach dem Vermissten,
an welcher sich ▆▆▆ Angehörige der Gendarmerie beteiligten,eingestellt
werden."Am Abend des gleichen Tages beendete ich meine Famulatur und
reiste zurück in die Hauptstadt,wo ich mein Studium fortsetzte.

Thomas Bernhard in front of the Fabjan family's apartment in 1966 (Salzburg, Radetzkystraße 10)

Thomas Bernhard, 1960s

Acceptance Speech for the ›Austrian State Prize‹ of 1968, typed manuscript

On the following pages: *Meine Preise/My Prizes*, typed manuscript

Meine Preise/My Prizes, an unpublished work of prose.
Bernhard describes the award ceremonies

Verehrter Herr Minister,

verehrte Anwesende,

es ist nichts zu leben, nichts zu verdammen, nichts anzuklagen, aber es ist vieles lächerlich; es ist alles lächerlich, wenn man den Tod bedenkt.

Man geht durch das Leben, beeindruckt, unbeeindruckt, durch die Szene, alles ist austauschbar, im Requisitenstaat besser oder schlechter geschult: ein Irrtum ! Man begreift: ein ahnungsloses Volk, ein schönes Land - es sind tote oder gewissenhaft gewissenlose Väter, Menschen mit der Einfachheit und der Niedertracht, mit der Armut ihrer Bedürfnisse...Es ist alles eine zuhöchst philosophische und unerträgliche Vorgeschichte.Die Zeitalter sind schwachsinnig, das Dämonische in uns ein immerwährender vaterländischer Kerker, in dem die Elemente der Dummheit und der Rücksichtslosigkeit zur tagtäglichen Notdurft geworden sind,Der Staat ist ein Gebilde, das fortwährend zum Scheitern, das Volk ein solches, das ununterbrochen zur Infamie und zur Geistesschwäche verurteilt ist.Das Leben Hoffnungslosigkeit, an die sich die Philosophien anlehnen, in welcher alles letztenende verrückt werden muss.

Wir sind Österreicher, wir sind apathisch; wir sind das Leben als das gemeine Desinteresse am Leben, wir sind in dem Prozess der Natur der Grössenwahn-Sinn als Zukunft.

Wir haben nichts zu berichten, als dass wir erbärmlich sind, durch Einbildungskraft einer philosophisch-ökonomisch-mechanischen Monotonie verfallen.

Mittel zum Zwecke des Niedergangs, Geschöpfe der Agonie, erklärt sich uns alles, verstehen wir nichts.Wir bevölkern ein Trauma, wir fürchten fürchten uns, wir haben ein Recht, uns zu fürchten, wir sehen schon, wenn

Der österreichische Staatspreis für Literatur

28

Den österreuchischen Staatspreis für Literatur habe ich neunzehnhundert-
siebenundsechzig bekommen und ich muss sofort sagen,dass es sich um den
sogenannten Kleinen Staatspreis handelte,den ein Schriftsteller nur für
eine bestimmte Arbeit bekommt und für den er sich selbst zu bewerben
hat,indem er eine seiner Arbeiten bei dem zuständigen Ministerium für
Kultur und Kunst einreicht und den ich in einem Alter bekommen habe,in
welchem man ihn normalerweise gar nicht mehr bekommt,nämlich wie ich in den fort-
geschrittenen Dreissigerjahren,wo es üblich geworden ist,diesen Preis
schon den Zwanzigjährigen zu geben,was absolut richtig ist,also dass es
sich um den sogenannten Kleinen Staatspreis handelte und nicht um den
sogenannten Grossen,der für ein sogenanntes Lebenswerk gegeben wird.Nie-
mand war mehr über die Tatsache verwundert,dass ich den kleinen Staatsprei
s verliehen bekommen habe,als ich selbst,denn ich hatte überhaupt
keine meiner Arbeiten eingereicht,ich hätte das niemals getan,ich hatte
davon nichts gewusst,dass mein Bruder,wie er mir später gestanden hatte,
am letzten Tag der Einreichungsfrist meinen Frost an der Pforte des Min-
isteriums für Kunst und Kultur auf dem Minoritenplatz abgegeben hatte.

Obkirchergasse,Grinzinger-Allee und fuhren in die Stadt hinein.Diese Fahrt
war die Fahrt zu einer Hinrichtung.Im sogenannten Audienzsaal des Kultur-und Kunst-und Unterrichtsministeriums fand die Preisverleihung statt.
Wie wir angekommen sind,waren schon alle sogenannten Ehrengäste anwesend.
Nur der Minister fehlte noch,Herr Piffl-Percevic,ein ehemaliger Sekretär
des steiermärkischen Landwirtschaftskammer mit einem Schnauzbart,der direk
t von seiner steiermärkischen Stellung als Minister in das Kultur-und Kunst-und Unter-
richtsministerium geholt worden war.Dieser Von seinem Parteifreund, der gerade Kanzler gewesen war war mir immer ein Greuel
gewesen,denn er konnte keinen einzigen Satz korrekt zuende sprechen und Piffl-Percevic
es mag sein,dass er etwas von steirischen Kälbern und Kühnen und von obersteirischen
Schweinen und von untersteirischen Mistbeeten verstand,von Kunst und Kul-
tur verstand er jedenfalls nichts.Aber das ist etwas Anderes.Der Minster obwohl er ununterbrochen und überall von Kunst und Kultur redete.
mit dem Schnauzbart kam in den Audienzsaal herein und die Preisverleihung
konnte beginnen.Der Minister hatte in der ersten Reihe Platz genommen,
in welcher die Preisanwärter sassen,fünf oder sechs ausser mir.Auch diese
Preisverleihung begann mit einem Musikstück,es war ein Streicherstück und
der Minister hörte es sich mit nach links geneigtem Kopf an.Die Musiker
waren nicht gut in Form und sie patzten an vielen Stellen,aber bei solchen
Gelegenheiten nicht einmal auf korrektes Spiel Wert gelegt werden.
Mich schmerzte es,dass die Musiker ausgerechnet an den besten Stellen des
Musikstückes patzten.Schliesslich war das Musikstück zuende und dem Minis-

aus der Rocktasche und verlas ihn,möglicherweise mit zittriger Stimme,
sein.Auch die Beine bebten mir,naturgemäss.Aber ich war noch nicht zuende
mit meinem Text,als der Saal unruhig wurde,ich wusste gar nicht warum,
denn mein Text war von mir ruhig gesprochen und das Thema war ein Philo-
sophisches,wenn auch von einiger Tiefgründigkeit,wie ich fühlte und ein
paarmal hatte ich das Wort Staat ausgesprochen.Ich dachte,das ist ein
ganz ruhiger Text,mit dem ich mich hier,weil ihn doch kaum jemand versteht
mehr oder weniger ohne Aufhebens aus dem Staub machen könne,vom Tod und
seiner Übermacht und von der Lächerlichkeit alles Menschlichen handelte
er von der Unfähigkeit und von der Sterblichkeit der Menschheit und von
der Nichtigkeit aller Staaten.Ich war mit meinem Text noch nicht zuende
gekommen,da war der Minister mit hochrotem Gesicht aufgesprungen und auf
mich zugerannt und hatte mir irgendein mir unverständliches Schimpfwort
an den Kopf geworfen.In höchster Erregung stand er vor mir und bedrohte mich
vor Wut.Ja,er ging mit erhobener Hand auf mich zu.Dann
auf mich zu,darauf eine abrupte
machte er zwei oder drei Schritte eine Kehrtwendung und verliess
den Saal.Zuerst war er ganz ohne Begleiter zur Glastür des Audienzsaals
gestürzt und hatte die Tür mit einem lauten Knall zugeworfen.Dies alles
geschah in Sekundenschnelle.Kaum hatte der Minister und über alles erbost eigenhändig die Tür
seines Audienzsaales hinter sich zugeworfen,war das Chaos im Saal.Das heisst,
zuerst,nachdem der Minister die Tür zugeworfen hatte,herrschte einen Augenblick betretene Stille.Dann war ein Chaos ausgebrochen.Ich selbst verstand überhaupt nicht,was geschehen war.Ich hatte hier eine Demütigung
nach der andern über mich ergehen lassen müssen und dann meinen,wie ich
glaubte,harmlosen Text vorgelesen und daraufhin erboste sich der
Minister und verliess wütend den Saalmund seine Vasallen gingen auf mich
los.Die ganze Meute im Saal,alles Leute,die von dem Minister abhängig

Es kommt in ein Altersheim,dachte ich.
Buffett geschehen wird.Der Minister hat dich
brüskiert,nicht umgekehrt,sagte einer meiner Freunde.Das war ein gutes
Wort.Er hat alle brüskiert,sagte ich.Der Minister hat die Audienzsaaltür
so zugeworfen,dass die Scheiben zersprungen sind,habe ich gedacht.Aber
als ich die Audienzsaaltür untersuchte,stellte sich heraus,dass keine
Scheibe zersprungen war.Es hatte sich nur so angehört,als seien die Scheiben der Audienzsaaltür zersprungen.Die Zeitungen schrieben am nächsten
Tag von einem Skandal,den der Schriftsteller Bernhard provoziert habe.Eine Wiener

Zeitung,die sich Wiener Montag nannte,schrieb auf der ersten Seite,ich
sei eine Wanze,die man vertilgen müsse.

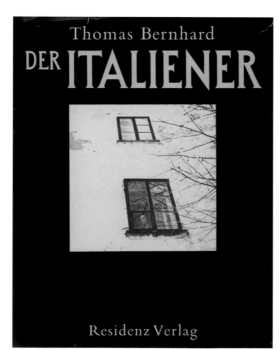

Der Italiener/The Italian,
handwritten draft of a movie script

Rewrite of a prose fragment, 1965.
Filmed by Ferry Radax at Wolfsegg castle

Thomas Bernhard

DER ITALIENER

Residenz Verlag

Der Italiener/The Italian,
Salzburg: Residenz 1971

Thomas Bernhard at the Attnang/Puchheim train station (Upper Austria)

Thomas Bernhard
in Nathal

Der Italiener/
The Italian,
typed manuscript

wald im Riental beschäftigt, während
der Italiener in Meditation, wie mir
vorkam, betroffen, schwieg.So viel ich weiss, war er seit seiner Ankunft nur immer
allein gewesen.er war kein gesprächiger Mensch.Unzugänglich.Er war für jetzt

für kurze Zeit zu kommen.und ab.Ich zeigte ihm die Theaterkostüme, die meine
ich sagte zu dem Italiener kopflos
Schwestern in Eile, bevor sie den Vater im Lusthaus aufbahrten,
jetzt waren sie schmutzig, vom Regen aufgeweicht.
für sich erkennbar,

sen, wer denn das Schauspiel,

Halbneun und halbelf,"wie auf den selbstgemalten Plakaten zu lesen

stand, die jetzt in dem Kostümhaufen lagen,geschrieben habe,ob es ein

tragisches oder ein lustiges sei,"vielleicht märchenhaft,"wie er

sagte.Ich antwortete,dass der älteste Sohn meiner jüngeren Schwester

der Dichter des Schauspiels sei,ich hätte es noch nicht gelesen,

Mensch habe es bis jetzt gelesen,ausser den Mitspielern,das sei eine

gute Idee. meinte ich,das Schauspiel noch heute im Bett zu lesen

Soviel ich wisse,sei es tragisch und lustig

zugleich.Da mir das Wesen dessen,der es geschrieben hat,meines ältest

n Neffen,nicht unbekannt sei, das Schauspiel sich gefallen.

"Es ist intelligenteste,"sagte ich und ich zog den Königs

aus dem Haufen heraus.Ich sagte dem Italiener,dass bei uns jedes

Jahr ein Schauspiel aufgeführt werde,immer ein von den

Kindern,meistens den Söhnen,selber geschriebenes,es sei erstaunlich,
Schwester mehr als zwei Dutzend!
wie gut diese Schauspiele immer seien,sogar von unseren

Grosseltern hätten wir immer noch welche,eines ist mir vom Lesen noch

in Erinnerung,es hat den Titel "Der Sperber";diese Schauspiele,

die,traditionsgemäss immer nur ein einziges Mal hier im Lusthaus

gespielt werden, eine Fundgrube für die Theaterwissenschafter,
sie einmal zum Mittelpunkt eines
selbst hätte Lust,
Aufsatzes zu machen; diese Schauspiele,Komödien wie auch Tragödien,

würden immer in einem einzigen Tag,in einer einzigen Nacht,geschriebe
bereits mit acht Jahren
n,ich selbst hätte ein solches verfasst;es sei

,sagte ich,der Einfluss unserer Mutterseite,das Italienische,das

die Familie zur Schauspielerei inspiriert habe; ich war froh,auf

diese Weise bei dem Italiener,der bis dahin immer sehr reserviert ge-
aufeinmal gewonnen
wesen war,einen freundlicheren, gesprächigeren Partner

zu haben;auch seine Familie hätte,bei ihm zuhause,in Florenz,oft

Theater gespielt,"mit Masken,"sagte er,meistens aber im Winter,im
merkwürdig,
Hause,in der Halle des Hauses,"nicht selbstverfasste,sondern Spiele

englischer Herkunft,von Shakeaspeare und Johnson,französische von

Moliere und Racine;alle diese Spiele,sagte er, in unser Lust-

haus,ob es zu dem Zweck,in ihm Theater zu spielen,gebaut worden sei?

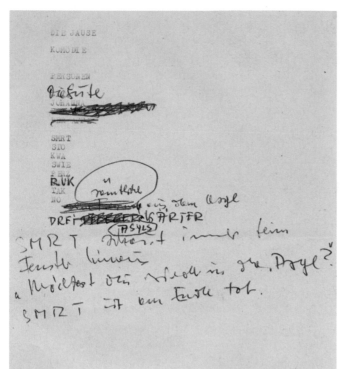

Ein Fest für Boris/A Party for Boris, early version (about 1967), still under its earlier title *Die Jause/The Snack*

Premiere in 1970 at the Deutsches Schauspielhaus in Hamburg; directed by Claus Peymann, Bernhard´s breakthrough as a playwright

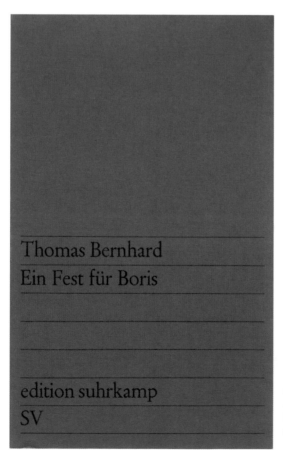

*Ein Fest für Boris/
A Party for Boris*,
Frankfurt am Main:
Suhrkamp 1970

THOMAS BERNHARD

~~Ein~~ Fest für Boris
~~DIE JAUSE~~

KOMÖDIE

1. Vorspiel

2. Vorspiel

das Fest

die gute, Johanna, Boris, ~~~~ die Krüppel
das Fehn beim Lose Krüppel
sämtliche, außer ~~~~ Johanna u. d. Krüppel,
in Rollstühlen

Boris alt u. klein (Säugling)
Johanna groß, stark, athletisch !

Krüppel: lustig, kindlich, lebensfroh,
karlotto, Emsteighart, u. a.

Thomas Bernhard
Mondsee 1969

Ein Fest für Boris/
A Party for Boris,
typed manuscript

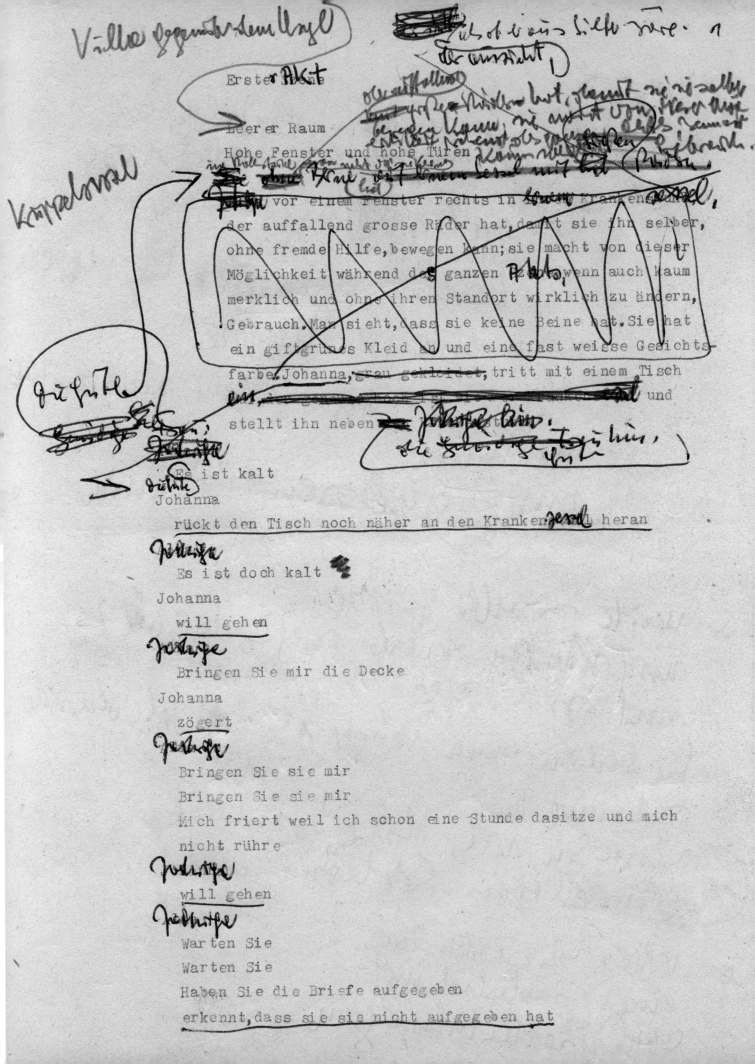

Erster Akt

Leerer Raum

Hohe Fenster und hohe Türen

vor einem Fenster rechts in ~~einem~~ Krankensessel,
der auffallend grosse Räder hat, damit sie ihn selber,
ohne fremde Hilfe, bewegen kann; sie macht von dieser
Möglichkeit während des ganzen ~~Akts~~ wenn auch kaum
merklich und ohne ihren Standort wirklich zu ändern,
Gebrauch. Man sieht, dass sie keine Beine hat. Sie hat
ein giftgrünes Kleid an und eine fast weisse Gesichts-
farbe. Johanna, grau gekleidet, tritt mit einem Tisch
ein, und
stellt ihn neben

Es ist kalt

Johanna

rückt den Tisch noch näher an den Kranken~~sessel~~ heran

Es ist doch kalt

Johanna

will gehen

Bringen Sie mir die Decke

Johanna

zögert

Bringen Sie sie mir

Bringen Sie sie mir

Mich friert weil ich schon eine Stunde dasitze und mich

nicht rühre

will gehen

Warten Sie

Warten Sie

Haben Sie die Briefe aufgegeben

erkennt, dass sie sie nicht aufgegeben hat

Thomas Bernhard,
Krucka (one of his
homes) 1977

Wie ich
Burgtheaterdirektor
werden sollte/
How I was supposed
to become manager
of the Burgtheater,
typed manuscript

theatralische
Die/Bruchbude auf dem Ring

für den Ja und Amensager aus dem Hause entschieden.

nach dem Telegr.nichts mehr gehört.
XXXXXXXXXXWXXXXXXXXXX Das war schäbig.Oder war es der
österreichische Charme ?

i n Deutschland ist schon alles ziemlich scheusslich,was mit
Kultur zu tun hat und es ist das meiste/verlogen Aber die
Meister XXXXXXXXXXXXXXXXXXXXXX Verlogenheit/und der Inkompe-
tenz und die Grossmeister der Intrige sitzen immer in Wien !

gegen diverse Falschmeldungen

Es war kein X künstlerisches Abendessen,in das der sogenannte Generalsekretär d.Bundestheaterverwaltung mit XXXXX/Stosseufzer,dass er noch
immer keinen Burgtheaterdirektor gefunden habe,sondern ein sogenannter
Schwarzer Kaffee im/XXXXXXXX Der Generalsekretär der Bundestheater-
verwaltung starte mich längere Zeit an und sagte plötzlich : ja,wollen
Sie es nicht werden ? XXXXXXXXXXXXXXXXXXXX Scherz geworden.Ich
hatte das Angebot auf keinen Fall ernst genommen,mich aber,zugegeben,
über die vom Generalsekretär/aufgezählten gerade aus der Wahl gepurzel-
ten Burgteaterdirektorskandidaten,zugegeben,durch und durch amüsiertX.
Mit dem Schwarzen Kaffee hatte ich auch den Scherz mit dem Burgtheater-
direktorsposten vergessen.Z,, meinem Erstaunen hatte der Bundestheater-
generalsekretär seinen Vorschlag,ich solle Burgtheaterdirektor werden,je-
doch ernst gemeint.Er kündigte seinen Besuch in meinem Haus in Ohlsdorf
an und kam mit einem XXXXX jener voller Explosivstoff,die uns jetzt
schon seit Jahrzehnten das Fürchten lehren.Der Generalsekretär erneuerte
sein Angebot solange,bis ich/schwach geworden war und es aufeinmal selbst
tatsächlich ernst genommen habe,eine Tatsache,die für das Durchsetzungs-
vermögen des Generalsekretärs spricht.Wer ein solches Haus(mein Ohlsdorfer Haus!) aufbauen und in Ordnung halten kann,kann auch as Burgtheater aufbauen und in Ordnung halten,sagte der Generalsekretär und huchte
sozusagen in demütigem Schwung durch die grossen weissgekalkten XXX
Räume.Ich ahnte,während der Generalsekretär Sprüche und Bilder an meinen
Ohlsdorfer Wänden bewundernd und tatsächlich mit,wie ich sagen muss,höchster
Intelligenz und Raffinesse kommentierend, schon nach seiner ausgeworfenen
Angel geschnappt hatte.Noch stand er da,der XXXXXX Direktormacher und
mit seinem köstlichen Angebot,während ich schon an dem Angelblut am Gaumen
würgte.Es gab kein Entrinnen.Ich war fest entschlossen,aus der theatra-
lischen Burchbude auf dem Ring wieder ein Theater zu machen.Schreibst du

Thomas Bernhard in the mid-1970s

Wie ich Burgtheaterdirektor werden sollte/How I was supposed to become manager of the Burgtheater, typed manuscript

1975: Discussions regarding Bernhard´s taking over the directorship of the Burgtheater take place.
Minister of Education then chooses Achim Benning

du halt ein paar Jahre weniger oder gar nichts und ~~XXXXXX~~ machst dich
über den deprimierenden Saustall Burgtheater,habe ich mir gedacht.~~XXX~~
Schliesslich ~~bist~~ du im besten Alter und hast,wie ich dachte,die besten
~~MMMMMMMMMMMMMMMMMMMMM~~
Voraussetzungen für dieses Abenteuer.Warum nicht der Einschub einer
urösterreichischen Groteske in deine Schriftstellerexistenz.Tatsächlich
beschäftigte ich mich nicht nur wochenlang,sondern monatelang mit der
sogenannten Erneuerung des Burgtheaters,wie ich sie mir vorstellte,mit
nichts anderem,ich war also tatsächlich dumm genug,das Angebot des Herrn
Gerealsekretärs ernst und immer ernster zu nehmen.Es gab noch mehrere
Zusammentreffen mit dem Generalsekretär,ihr Inhalt war ja nur immer ~~XX~~
intensiver auf nur ein Ziel hin gewesen: dass ich also zum Burgtheaterdirek
tor gemacht ~~werden solle~~.Tatsächlich muss ich damals wahnsinnig gewesen
sein !Der Herr Generalsekretär war begeistert,als er erfuhr,dass der seit
über einem
Jahrzehnt~~XX~~ nicht nur bei Gallimard/und Knopf in New York etcetera,auch
noch ein ordentliches Studium als Schauspieler und Regisseur an einer
österreichischen Hochschule abgeschlossen und ~~XX~~ sogar die sogenannte Ge-
werkschaftsprüfung vor einer siebzehnköpfigen Kommission abgelegt hat.
Der Generalsekretär führte mich durch seine Räume in der Goethegasse,als
hätte er den neuen Burgtheaterdirektor schon in der Hand, ~~jedenfalls am Arm~~
Derweil hatte er ihn,wie ich später erfahren musste,nur auf den Arm genommen.
schon durch die Kulissendepots am Arsenal und durch die Malersäle und
stellte mich den Leuten dort vor und ~~es führte mich~~
schon
Als der ~~XXXX~~ sich seiner Sache mit dem Bernhard~~XXXXX~~/sichere Generalse-
im Burgtheater selbst eine Umfrage startete,ob Bernhard oder nicht,
kretär ~~XXXXXXXXXXXXXXXXXXXXXXXXXXXXXXXXXXXXXXXXXXXXXX~~
hatten schlagartig
~~XXXXXX,XXXXXXXXXXXXXXXXXXXXXXXXXXXXXXXX~~Achtundneunzig Prozent des
(selbstverständlich!)
Ensembles ~~XXXXX~~/gegen Bernhard~~XXXXXXXXX~~ gestimmt.Der Sauhaufen sollte ~~XXX~~
nicht angerührt,die ~~XXX~~theatralische Bruchbude bestehen bleiben.Der Ge-
bleiben
neralsekretär,der viele Monate so eifrig hinter mir her gewesen war und
mich letztenendes monatelang am Schreiben und also an meiner leidenschaft-
lichen Kunst gehindert hat,liess nmichts mehr hören.Er hatte sich,im Ein-
verständnis mit seinem Minister für den bekannten Ja-und Amensager aus de~~M~~
theaTRAlischen
Hause und also aus dem Saustall der Bruchbude entschieden.Ich hörte ganz
einfach nichts mehr und bekam eines Tages untenstehendes Telegramm.Das
war ärgerlich,weil es schäbig war.Oder war es der österreichische Charme?

Telegramm
dutzendmal
~~und der seine~~ Theaterstücke verhindert,als zugelassen und der seine The
aterstücke allein aus Selbsterhaltungstrieb schon seit über zehn Jahre~~n~~
auf Anfrage jederzeit
für Wien restlos gesperrt hat,wie sein Verlag bestätigen wird

Die Macht der Gewohnheit/The Force of Habit, draft

Thomas Bernhard

Die Macht
der Gewohnheit

Bibliothek Suhrkamp

Die Macht der Gewohnheit/
The Force of Habit,
Frankfurt am Main: Suhrkamp 1974

128

Wohnwagen Caribaldis

Ein Klavier links, ein Bett rechts, ~~darüber ein Portrait~~ ~~Franz~~
Kasten, Tisch, ~~mehrere~~ Sessel, Bilder, Spiegel.
~~Zwei~~ Notenständer vorn.

Auf dem Boden Das Forellenquintett.

[handschriftlich:] Caribaldi:
Jongleur: Hoft

[handschriftlich rechts:] Caribaldi: ~~Kunstdirektor~~
Jongleur
Dompteur
Spaßmacher
Seiltänzerin

[handschriftlich:] Motto

[handschriftlich:]

Unglaublich
hinaus mit dir
mach deine Spässe

[handschriftlich unten:] Hoft holt den Direktor noch seines Lebens

Thomas Bernhard, Sicily (Mt. Etna) 1977

Die Macht der Gewohnheit/The Force of Habit, typed manuscript

[handwritten top:] Alle ... ...
Sesseln an Notenständer

Carib.   Crescendo

wenn ich crescendo sage

decreszendo

[handwritten] ... ich decrescendo *[struck through]*

Diese Notenständer *[handwritten annotations]*

[handwritten:] Die Notenständer

sind alle zu kurz

[struck through handwriting]

Unbeweglich Notenständer

völlig unbewegliche

Seit zehn Jahren

wünsche ich

unbewegliche Notenständer

andere Sessel

die nicht knarren *[handwritten:]* ... Sessel ... ...

zur Enkelin

Das ist ganz gut

immer wieder
    ein
Opus/hundertvierzehn

Allegro vivace

also

forte

pianissimo

crescendo

forte
      zum Jongleur
keine Verzögerungen

Aber wir können nicht anfangen

solange mein Neffe nicht da ist
macht einen tiefen Ton auf d.Cello

Jongleur

streicht die Geige

Enkelin

streicht die Viola

Carib. zur Enkelin

crescendo

verstehst du

Würsteholen XXXNXXXbeim Noppinger in Maxglan
Kinogänge Maxglan etc.
Zentral,wo oben d.Englischlehrerin aus Hannover war
alles Th.W.Werner.

Geige im Schuhkammerl,Gestank

Blick auf Sebastiansfriedhof

Luftmine in Schranne/Ohrfeige

Alarm in d.Nacht,ich stehe auf,gehe aufs Klo und lege mich wieder

ins Bett.Ohrfeige.

Stiefel auf den Kachelofen nach dem Krieg.
zum Laufen Hitlerjugend nach Gnigl.Siegernagel.

Fünfmarkstück Weihnachten verloren,März gefunden.

Die Ursache/An Indication of the Cause, draft

Die Ursache/
An Indication of the Cause,
Salzburg: Residenz 1975

Franz Wesenauer, a parish priest in Salzburg, felt he had
been brought into discredit as ›Onkel Franz‹ (›Uncle Franz‹)
in the first volume of Bernhard's autobiography and sued
the author; the text of all later editions corresponds to the
court's decision taken at Salzburg Regional Court in 1977

Die Tittorode

I. ~~...~~ [Überschrift gestrichen]

I. ...kreuz | ... | letzte die (Umgebung / Straßen
II. Onkel Franz | Koblenz | | Gehen etc.

Gegenüber, englische, denn 45 Güterlager,
Zeichnen (alter Mann mit Papierbogen im Alten...) ...
... (Preis-) engl., Franz. | gegen einen ... ...
... etc. PANZER ... dem Haus (...
..., Tiger hinten.

Plünderung | ... , rote Fahnen, Amerikaner
etc.

... kreuz = Onkel Franz (...)

Weist | ... ...

... Großvater, denn 35 Betten. | Blumen
... ...gasse etc.

... Leopoldskron, alte morsches Holz

...gen ... kreuz ... weg

→ ... sagt immer das ist die
FÜR Sache

Thomas Bernhard, Sicily 1977

An Indication of the Cause, typed manuscript

Schluss Ursache

..... hatte ich einen Mitschüler,der hatte nur einen Arm,den linken und
der leere Ärmel war in seine linke Rocktasche gesteckt.Jeden Tag
läutete ich an der Haustür des Einarmigen,der ein anständiger und
hochbegabter Kerl gewesen war,ein guter Freund und ein disziplinier-
ter Charakter, und [...] wartete,bis er [...] *angekündigt durch seine immer gleichen,*
von seiner Mutter immer auf die gleiche adrette Weise frisiert,
rhythmischen Schritte schon im Vorhaus erschien und ging mit ihm
Mann
das letzte Drittel der Reichenhallerstrasse und durch das Neutor
ab sofort nicht mehr in das Gymnasium zu gehen, und ich läutete nicht an der
in das Gymnasium.Eines Tages,ich war gerade sechzehn gewesen,beschlo-
/Zwischen meinem Zuhause u. d. Hause des Einarmigen [...]
ss ich,[...]
Haustür des Einarmigen und ich ging aufeinmal,[...],nachdem
ich allein durchs Neutor gegangen war,nicht ins Gymnasium,das ich
hasste,sondern mit aufeinmal unglaublich schnellen Schritten salzach-
auf der Lehrstellenvermittlung
abwärts bis zur Lehener Brücke und in das Arbeitsamt,[...]
[...]
[...]
[...]
[...]

und eine solche war mir innerhalb [M]einer Stunde in nächster Nähe de[s]
bei einem Lebensmittelhändler
Arbeitsamtes in der Scherzhauserfeldsiedlung vermittelt gewesen.Zu-
hause sagte ich,ich ginge von jetzt an nicht mehr auf das Gymnasium,
sondern zu einem Lebensmittelhändler in der Schwerzhauserfeldsiedlun[g]
Ich ging auf den Dachboden und stellte die Schultasche mit dem ge-
in die Lehre.[...]
gehassten Inhalt in einen Winkel und kaufte mir einen grauen Ge-
schäftsmantel.

/ Es war ihnen gleichgültig,was ich machte.

Ende

Thomas Bernhard

Holzfällen
Eine Erregung

Während alle auf den Schauspieler warteten,der ihnen versprochen
hatte,nach der Premiere der _Wildente_ gegen halbzwölf zu ihrem Abendessen in die Gentzgasse zu kommen,beobachtete ich die Auersberger
genau von jenem Ohrensessel aus,in welchem ich in den fünfziger-und
in den ersten sechziger Jahren beinahe täglich gesessen war und
dachte,dass es ein gravierender Fehler gewesen ist,die Einladung der
Auersberger anzunehmen.Zwanzig Jahre hatte ich die Auersberger nicht
mehr gesehen und ausgerechnet am Todestag unserer gemeinsamen Freundin _Joana_ habe ich sie auf dem Graben getroffen und ohne Umschweife
habe ich ihre Einladung zu ihrem _künstlerischen Abendessen_,so die
auersbergerischen Eheleute über ihr ~~Nachtmahl~~,angenommen.Zwanzig
Jahre habe ich von den Eheleuten Auersberger nichts mehr wissen
wollen und zwanzig Jahre habe ich die Eheleute Auersberger nicht mehr
gesehen und in diesen zwanzig Jahren hatten mir die Eheleute Auers-

Holzfällen/Woodcutters, typed manuscript

Holzfällen/Woodcutters,
Frankfurt am Main: Suhrkamp 1984

1984: Gerhard Lampersberg believes he has been
brought into discredit and has copies of the book
confiscated

fürchtete Wollzeile und die Operngasse, auf welcher ich so oft in die Falle gerade jener Menschen gegangen bin, die ich immer am meisten gehasst habe. Aber in den letzten Wochen, dachte ich auf dem Ohrensessel, hatte ich aufeinmal ein grosses █████████ Bedürfnis gehabt, gerade auf den Graben und auf die Kärntnerstrasse zu gehen, wegen der guten Luft und dem mir vormittägigen aufeinmal angenehmen ███████████ Menschenwirbel dort und gerade auch auf dem Graben und auf der Kärntnerstrasse, wahrscheinlich, weil ich endlich und entschieden monatelangen Döblinger also meiner Alleinsein in meiner Wohnung █████ tödlichen Einsamkeitskrankheit) dem entkommen wollte. Ich habe es in den letzten Wochen immer als grossen Genuss empfunden, die Kärnterstrasse und den Graben entlang und also hin und wieder den Graben und die Kärntnerstrasse zurück zu gehen, meinem Kopf hat dieses Hinunhergehen genauso gut getan, wie meinem Körper; als ob ich in letzter Zeit dieses Hinunhergehen auf dem Graben und auf der Kärntnerstrasse wie nichts notwendig gehabt hätte, lief ich tagtäglich in den letzten Wochen die Kärntnerstrasse und den Graben hinauf und wieder hinunter; auf der Kärntnerstrasse und auf dem Graben war ich aufeinmal █████ monatelänger █████████ wieder offen gesagt, nach Geistes-und Körperschwäche, in Schwung gekommen; es erfrischte mich █████████ wenn ich die Kärnterstrasse hinauflief und den Graben und wieder zurück; nur dieses Hinundherlaufen, habe ich dabei immer gedacht und es ist doch mehr gewesen; nur dieses Hinundherlaufen sagte ich mir immer wieder und es hat mich tatsächlich wieder denken und tatsächlich wieder philosophieren lassen, mich ████████ wieder mit Philosophie und mit Literatur beschäftigen lassen, die in mir schon so lange Zeit unterdrückt, ja abgetötet █ gewesen waren. Gerade dieser lange Winter hat in mir alles Literarische und alles Philosophische abgetötet gehabt, dachte ich auf dem Ohrensessel, durch dieses Hinundherlaufen auf dem Graben und auf der Kärntnerstrasse habe ich es mir selbst wieder zum Leben erweckt, ███████████████ und ich führte tatsächlich als meinen derzeitigen Geisteszustand, der aufeinmal ein sozusagen geretteter Geisteszustand bezeichnet werden darf, auf diese Graben-Kärntnerstrasseterapie zurück, die ich mir verordnet hatte ab Mitte Jänner. Diese entsetzliche Stadt Wien, dachte ich, die mich tief in die Verzweiflung und tatsächlich wieder einmal an den Rand des völligen Ruins gebracht hat, ist plötzlich der Motor, der meinen Kopf wieder in Gang bringt, der meinen Körper wieder zum Leben erweckt, von Tag zu Tag beobachtete ich in Kopf und Körper die fortschreitende Wiederbelebung alles dessen, was in mir den ganzen Winter über schon abgestorben gewesen war; hatte ich den ganzen Winter über immer wieder Wien die Schuld an meinem geistigen und körperlichen Absterben gegeben, so war es jetzt dasselbe Wien, dem ich meine Wiederbelebung verdankte. Ich sass auf dem Ohrensessel und lobte also die Kärnterstrasse und den Graben und führte meine geistige und körperliche Wiederherstellung auf diese meine Kärntnerstrassen-und Grabenterapie zurück, auf nichts sonst und ich sagte mir, dass ich naturgemäss für diese erfolgreiche Terapie einen Preis zu zahlen habe und dachte, dass ████

Thomas Bernhard,
Ottnang 1988

Thomas Bernhard

[Holzfällen]
Eine Erregung

Da ich nun einmal nicht imstande
war,die Menschen vernünftiger zu
machen,war ich lieber fern von
ihnen glücklich. Voltaire

Während alle auf den Schauspieler warteten,der ihnen versprochen hatte,
nach der Premiere der Wildente gegen halbzwölf zu ihrem Abendessen in die
Gentzgasse zu kommen,beobachtete ich die Eheleute Auersberger genau von
jenem Ohrensessel aus,in welchem ich in den frühen/fünfziger Jahren beinahe täglich gesessen war und dachte,dass es ein gravierender Fehler gewesen ist,
die Einladung der Auersberger anzunehmen.Zwanzig Jahre hatte ich die Auersberger nicht mehr gesehen und ausgerechnet am Todestag unserer gemeinsamen
Freundin Joana habe ich sie auf dem Graben getroffen und ohne Umschweife
habe ich ihre Einladung zu ihrem künstlerischen Abendessen,so die auersbergerischen Eheleute über ihr Nachtmahl,angenommen.Zwanzig Jahre habe ich
von den Eheleuten Auersberger nichts mehr wissen wollen und zwanzig Jahre
habe ich die Eheleute Auersberger nicht mehr gesehen und in diesen zwanzig
Jahren hatten mir die Eheleute Auersberger allein bei Nennung ihres Namens
durch Dritte Übelkeit verursacht,dachte ich auf dem Ohrensessel,und jetzt
konfrontieren mich die Eheleute Auersberger mit ihren und mit meinen Fünf-
zigerjahren.Zwanzig Jahre bin ich den Eheleuten Auersberger aus dem Weg gegangen,zwanzig Jahre habe ich sie nicht ein einziges Mal getroffen und ausgerechnet jetzt habe ich ihnen auf dem Graben begegnen müssen,dachte ich;
dass es tatsächlich eine verheerende Dummheit gewesen ist,gerade an diesem
Tag auf den Graben zu gehen und auch noch,wie es meine Gewohnheit geworden ist allerdings seit ich aus London nach Wien zurückgekommen bin,auch
noch auf dem Graben mehrere Male hin und her zu gehen,wo ich es mir hätte
ausrechnen können,dass ich die Auersberger einmal treffen muss,und nicht
nur die Auersberger,sondern auch alle anderen von mir in den letzten Jahrzehnten gemiedenen Leute,mit welchen ich in den fünfziger Jahren einen in-
tensiven,wie die Auersberger zu sagen pflegten,intensiven künstlerischen
Verkehr gehabt habe;den ich aber schon vor einem Vierteljahrhundert aufgegeben habe,also genau zu dem Zeitpunkt,in welchem ich von den Auersberger
weg nach London gegangen bin,weil ich mit allen diesen Wiener Leuten von
damals gebrochen habe,wie gesagt wird,sie nicht mehr sehen und mit ihnen absolut nichts mehr zu tun haben wollte.Auf den Graben gehen heisst ja nichts
anderes,als direkt in die Wiener Gesellschaftshölle zu gehen und gerade jene
Leute zu treffen,die ich nicht treffen will,deren Auftauchen mir auch heute
noch alle möglichen Körper-und Geisteskrämpfe verursacht,dachte ich auf dem
Ohrensessel sitzend und ich hatte aus diesem Grunde schon in den letzten Jahren
meiner Wienbesuche von London aus den Graben gemieden und bin andere Wege
gegangen,auch nicht auf den Kohlmarkt,selbstverständlich auch nicht auf
die Kärntnerstrasse,die Spiegelgasse habe ich gemieden genauso wie die
Stallburggasse und die Dorotheergasse und ebenso die von mir immer ge-

Auslöschung/Extinction, handwritten draft on the instructions of a washing machine

Auslöschung/Extinction,
Frankfurt am Main: Suhrkamp 1986

1986: last novel appears
although written in 1981

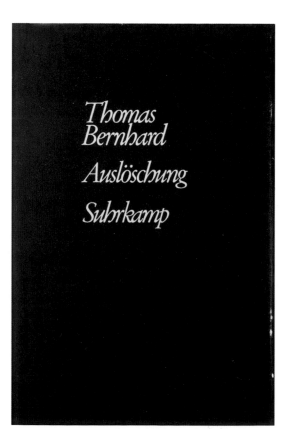

Nach der Unterredung mit meinem Schüler Gambetti,mit welchem ich mich
am Neunundzwanzigsten auf dem Pincio getroffen habe,schreibt ~~Pöttinger~~,
um die Mai-Termine für den Unterricht zu vereinbaren und von dessen
hoher Intelligenz ich auch jetzt nach meiner Rückkehr aus Wolfsegg ü-
berrascht,ja in einer derart erfrischenden Weise begeistert gewesen bin,
dass ich ganz gegen meine Gewohnheit,gleich durch die Via Condotti auf
die Piazza Minerva zu gehen,auch in dem Gedanken,tatsächlich schon lange
in Rom und nicht mehr in Österreich zuhause zu sein,in eine zunehmend
heitere Stimmung versetzt,über die Flaminia und die Piazza del Popolo,
den ganzen Corso entlang in meine Wohnung gegangen bin,erhielt ich gegen zwei Uhr mittag das Telegramm,in welchem mir der Tod meiner Eltern
und meines Bruders Johannes mitgeteilt wurde.<u>Eltern und Johannes tödlich verunglückt.Caecilia,Amalia.</u> Das Telegramm in Händen,trat ich
ruhig und mit klarem Kopf an das Fenster meines Arbeitszimmers und schau-
te auf die vollkommen menschenleere Piazza Minerva hinunter.Ich hatte
Gambetti fünf Bücher gegeben,von welchen ich überzeugt gewesen bin,dass
sie ihm für die nächsten Wochen nützlich und notwendig sein werden und
ihm aufgetragen,diese fünf Bücher auf das Aufmerksamste und mit der in
seinem Falle gebotenen Langsamkeit zu studieren: <u>Siebenkäs</u> von Jean Paul,
<u>Der Prozess</u> von Franz Kafka, ~~Amras von Thomas Bernhard~~ <u>Die Portugiesin</u>
von Musil,<u>Esch oder Die Anarchie</u> von Broch und dachte jetzt,nachdem ich
das Fenster geöffnet hatte,um besser atmen zu können,dass meine Entschei-
dung richtig gewesen war,Gambetti gerade diese fünf Bücher zu geben und
keine andern,weil sie im Laufe unseres Unterrichts ihm immer wichtiger
sein werden,dass ich ganz unauffällig die Andeutung gemacht habe,mich
das nächste Mal mit ihm über die <u>Wahlverwandtschaften</u> und nicht über
<u>Die Welt als Wille und Vorstellung</u> auseinanderzusetzen.Mit Gambetti zu
sprechen,war mir auch an diesem Tag wieder ein grosses Vergnügen gewesen nach den mühevollen,schwerfälligen,nur auf die alltäglichen ganz
und gar privaten und primitiven Bedürfnisse beschränkten Unterhaltungen
mit der Familie in Wolfsegg.Die deutschen Wörter hängen wie Bleigewichte
an der deutschen Sprache,sagte ich zu Gambetti und drücken in jedem Fall
den Geist auf eine diesem Geist schädliche Ebene.Das deutsche Denken wie
das deutsche Sprechen erlahmen sehr schnell unter der menschenunwürdigen
Last seiner Sprache,die alles Gedachte,noch bevor es überhaupt ausgespro-
chen wird,unterdrückt;unter der deutschen Sprache habe sich das deutsche
Denken nur schwer entwickeln und niemals zur Gänze entfalten können im
Gegensatz zum romanischen Denken unter den romanischen Sprachen,wie die
Geschichte der

---

* Geboren 1934 in Wolfsegg,gestorben 1981 in Rom.

Thomas Bernhard,
Nathal 1988

der Trauergäste mehr anzutreffen.Während ~~der darauffolgenden~~ Zeit hatte ich darüber
nachgedacht,was ich aus Wolfsegg machen werde,das,wie inzwischen ein-
wandfrei festgestellt worden war,ausschliesslich mir gehörte,<u>mit allen
Rechten und Pflichten</u>,wie juristisch gesagt wird.Ich hatte schon einen
Plan für die Zukunft von Wolfsegg im Kopf,als ich mich mit den Schwestern,ohne den Schwager daran teilnehmen zu lassen,was ich mir ausdrück-
lich verboten hatte,über die Zukunft von Wolfsegg unterhalten habe bis
zwei Uhr früh.Am Ende der Unterhaltung konnte ich den Schwestern nicht
sagen,was mit Wolfsegg geschehen wird,obwohl ich es zu diesem Zeitpunkt
schon gewusst habe,ich sagte ihnen,die mir während der ganzen Unterredung nichts zu sagen,aber doch immer ihre spöttischen und verbitterten
Gesichter gezeigt hatten,ich wisse nicht,was mit Wolfsegg geschieht,ich
hätte nicht die geringste Vorstellung in dieser Frage,während ich doch
gleichzeitig fest entschlossen war,mich bei Eisenberg in Wien anzumelden
auf ein Gespräch,in welchem ich ihm <u>ganz Wolfsegg,wie es liegt und steht,
und alles Dazugehörende</u>,als ein völlig bedingungsloses Geschenk an die
Israelitische Kultusgemeinde in Wien anbieten wollte.Dieses Gespräch
habe ich schon zwei Tage nach dem Begräbnis mit Eisenberg geführt und
Eisenberg hat ein Geschenk im Namen der Israelitischen Kultusgemeinde
angenommen.Von Rom aus,wo ich jetzt wieder bin und wo ich diese <u>Auslö-
schung</u> geschrieben habe,und wo ich bleiben werde,schreibt Röttinger,
dankte ich ihm ~~für die~~ Annahme.

1981 / 1986

X Leben 1934 in Wolfsegg,gestorben 1981 in Rom

das österreichische Volk ist
leicht missbrauchbar
es existiert heute noch ganz und gar
im Unterdrückungsmechanismus der Monarchie
und des Dritten Reiches

die Österreicher insgesamt als Masse
sind heute ein brutales und dummes Volk

Heldenplatz, draft

Heldenplatz,
Frankfurt am Main: Suhrkamp 1988

1988: fierce public debate on Bernhard's play
Heldenplatz, premiered at the Vienna Burgtheater in
the so-called ›Bedenkjahr‹ (= year of reflection): 50th
anniversary of Nazi annexation of Austria

Thomas Bernhard

Heldenplatz

Bibliothek Suhrkamp

144

following pages: *Heldenplatz*, typed manuscript

Kann schon sein dass Sie sich ein paarmal im Jahr
in dieser Stadt wohlfühlen
wenn Sie über den Kohlmarkt gehen oder über den Graben
oder die Singerstrasse hinunter in der Frühlingsluft

Thomas Bernhard,
Ottnang 1988

mich wundert es ja geradezu dass/ ~~längst~~ (nicht das ganze österreichische Volk
~~längst~~ Selbstmord gemacht hat

das wundert mich das wundert mich

In dieser Stadt müsste ein Sehender ja

tagtäglich rund um die Uhr Amok laufen

er schaut in Richtung auf das Burgtheater

Was diesem armen unmündigen Volk geblieben ist

ist nichts als das Theater

Österreich selbst ist nichts als eine Bühne

auf der alles verlottert und vermodert und verkommen ist

~~eine~~ in sich selber verhasste Statisterie

von sechseinhalb Millionen Alleingelassenen

sechseinhalb Millionen Debile und Tobsüchtige

die/aus vollem Hals ununterbrochen nach einem Regisseur schreien

Der Regisseur wird kommen

und sie endgültig in den Abgrund hinunterstossen

Sechseinhalb Millionen Statisten

die von ein paar verbrecherischen Hauptdarstellern

die die Hofburg und den Ballhausplatz bevölkern

an jedem Tag vor den Kopf

und am Ende doch wieder nur in den Abgrund gestossen werden

Die Österreicher sind ja nichts anderes

als vom Unglück besessene

der Österreicher ist von Natur aus unglücklich

und ist er einmal glücklich schämt er sich dessen

und versteckt sein Glück in seiner Verzweiflung

Anna   Der Vater hat schon alles richtig gesehen

der Vater ist immer konsequent gewesen

Professor Robert   Sich aus dem Fenster zu stürzen

ist auch keine Lösung

wenn es auch was euren Vater betrifft

die Konsequenz ~~gewesen ist~~

Euer Vater hat nie einen Ausweg gesehen

Ich gehe ganz einfach nicht mehr unter die Menschen

ich gehe nicht mehr unter die Menschen

und höre also nicht was sie sagen

und ich sehe ihre Fratzen nicht

euer Vater hat es aber ohne Menschen nicht ausgehalten

ich war stark genug nach Neuhaus zu gehn

euer Vater war dazu nicht imstande

Wahrscheinlich wäre er in Oxford total gescheitert

das Oxford von neunzehnhundertachtundachtzig

ist ja nicht mehr das Oxford von neunzehnhundert-
siebenundfünfzig

die Engländer haben auch einen faschistischen Unter-
satz

das wird immer vergessen

auch die Engländer haben ihren Faschismus

Thomas Bernhard,
Ottnang 1988

DIE SCHWERHÖRIGEN
Tragödie
~~Hans~~ Von
/ Urheber, Privatphilosoph redet über alles.

Lankaster, Brückenbauingenieur redet über Brücken etc.

Frau von Still, Private

Scherrer, Hosenkaufmann

Mager, Angestellter einer Versicherung

Frech, Speditionsgehilfe

Zadel, Museumsdiener

Alle, bis auf Frech und Zadel, über achtzig

Wartezimmer einer

/ Hals-Nasen-und Ohrenordination in Döbling (Währing?)

Frau v.Still hat sich einen riesigen Koffer gekauft, und tritt damit auf, mit dem
sie nach Cascais reisen will. Sie muss nur noch eine Ohrenkon-
trolle machen.
Mager ist Liebhaber von Zuckerbäckerei und malt Ansichten.

Frech geht fischen
Scherrer interessieren nur die Geschäfte
Zadel spricht über Velasquez.

Die Schwerhörigen/The Hard of Hearing, typed manuscript of an unpublished play

*Alle bis auf Friede und Tod [?]
über achtzig!* (handwritten)

Erste Szene

~~Ein Tisch,~~ Eine lange Bank, vier Sessel, ein Kleiderständer, ein Tisch mit Zeitschriften
halbacht Uhr früh
  selbstverständlich mit Hörgeräten.

Urheber und Lankaster / sitzend, *[handwritten insertion]*

Urheber bindet sich unter grössten Schwierigkeiten das rechte

    Schuhband fest

Lankaster / *mit Stolz* Ende November sagten Sie

    lauter

     Sie sagten Ende November

     Die Leute fahren ja schon Ende Oktober in den Süden

     sobald es hier kalt ist

     Heute haben alle Geld

     Alle opponieren und haben Geld

     Selbst die Hilfsarbeiter reisen

     heute an den ~~Südküsten~~ *[corrected]*

Urheber Ich streite nicht mit meiner Familie

     äusserste Zurückhaltung müssen Sie wissen

     Natürlich gehen mir meine Leute auf die Nerven

     ich habe es mir abgewöhnt

     mich unbedingt durchsetzen zu wollen
     neue Schuhe sind eine Tortur
     Bücken ist eine Katastrophe für mich

Lankaster Alle halten so viel auf die Meeresluft

     dabei ist die Meeresluft für die meisten schlecht

     Ich selbst vertrage ja auch die Meeresluft nicht

     Mein Zustand verschlimmert sich

     wenn ich mich der Meeresluft aussetze
     die Gehörgänge betreffend
     Mit acht Jahren bin ich zum erstenmal

     an die Ostsee gereist

Urheber vielleicht wäre eine halbe Nummer grösser
     besser gewesen.
Lankaster Damals reisten noch wenige ans Meer

     nur die die Geld hatten

     Wir hatten Geld

     mein Grossvater war ~~ein sogenannter~~ Grosskaufmann
     ~~wie sie wissen~~

     der die Meeresfische in Österreich eingeführt hat ~~sozusagen~~

     er hat einen für die Meeresfischeimportation geeigneten

     Waggon entworfen

     übrigens mit einem Herrn Eiffel zusammen

     Mein Grossvater war schon mit achtzehn Jahren in Moskau

     mit zweiundzwanzig machte er seine erste Südamerikareise
     Die Grossväter sind die Lehrmeister
     die Grossväter mütterlicherseits

Urheber Mit einer gewissen Schamlosigkeit

bin ich vorgegangen zweifellos

Weniger Rücksichtnahme im Alter naturgemäss

Lankaster Mein Grossvater lehrte mich mehr oder weniger alles

Ich habe fast alles von meinem Grossvater

mütterlicherseits

später habe ich nichts mehr gelernt

Die Menschen haben mich dann nurmehr noch abgestossen

Urheber In Paris lebte ich nocheinmal auf

eine Damenbekanntschaft

Rumänin Prinzessin alter Adel

plötzlich reizte mich auch das nicht mehr

Lankaster Ende November sagten Sie

richtet sich auf

Die Schwerhörigkeit kam bei meinem Grossvater

erst mit neunzig

meine Grossmutter mütterlicherseits

hat bis zuletzt ein absolut gutes Gehör

In Friedrichshafen lernte sie den Grafen Zeppelin
kennen

Lakehurst Sie wissen was ich meine

Die menschlichen Anstrengungen enden immer

mit einer Katastrophe

Glauben Sie dass mir die Insel Sylt hilft

ich glaube nicht dass mir die Insel Sylt hilft

Die Frage ist immer dieselbe

zu welchem Arzt

haben wir einen Arzt

sehen wir in der kürzesten Zeit

dass wir wieder in eine Falle gegangen sind

Ist Maulundklauenseuche ansteckend

ich meine können sich Menschen anstecken

an der Maulundklauenseuche

sehr laut zu Urheber

ich sagte ob sich Menschen an der Maulundklauenseuche

anstecken können

Urheber Die Schwierigkeit ist ja

dass Sie sich entscheiden müssen

gehen Sie zu dem einen Arzt

oder zu dem andern

Lankaster laut Ich sagte ob Maulundklauenseuche

für Menschen ansteckend ist

Thomas Bernhard,
Portugal (Sintra) 1987

Matterhorn, Kara-
korum, Neufund-
land/Newfoundland.
late drafts

Thomas Bernhard

Tho   Matterhorn

    Matterhorn

Der Verunglückte in Schlaugenham.Mannesmann etc.Schloss

                    Thomas Bernhard
                    Karakorum

Der eine Bruder ist Philosoph,der andere Arzt(der abgestürzte)
    geborene Mannesmann
die Mutter/versauft sich,der Vater ist Kartonindustrieller.

Stück: aus dem Arsch kommen alle Darsteller heraus.Politi er etc.

                    Thomas Bernhard
                    Neufundland
                    Roman
            Millemer sagte.Quarry sagte etc.Zwei sagen immer
            unter Umständen sogar das gerade Gegenteil.Das ist die
    Thomas Bernhard   totale Struktur in Schlaugenham.
                    Neufundland

Thomas Bernhard
Neufundland

Wenn wir einen tatsächlich nur seiner Arbeit lebenden,ja nur aus dieser
seiner Arbeit heraus existierenden Bruder als Internisten haben,entgehen
wir im Laufe der XXXX Jahrzehnte Hunderten von Ärzten,zu welchen uns die
Krankheit,die wir jetzt schon ein Vierteljahrhundert haben,naturgemäss
                              ohne einen solchen Bruder als Internisten
rücksichtslos getrieben hätte und wir wären/den/zum Grossteil ja doch
immer wieder nur gemeinen und skrupellosen und stumpfsinnigen medizini-
                          lebenslänglich   gewesen   und von
schen Geschäftemachern sozusagen/mit Haut und Haaren ausgeliefert/gewesen
ihnen belogen und betrogen und mit der grössten Wahrscheinlichkeit längst
vernichtet worden,sagte ich mir auf dem Weg zu meinem Haus.

    beim Wirt hohensinn Würste eingekauft im Rucksack zum Haus etc...
    Maschinpapier,Orangen etcetera...
    für drei Tage und drei Personen
mit den/notwendigen Lebensmitteln,dazu mit Würsten aus der/Fleischerei
in unseren Rucksäcken
hohensinn/ausgestattet,gingen mein Bruder und ich am vierundzwanzigsten
auf unser sogenanntes Forsthaus zu, das wir vor siebzehn Jahren von unserem
"aus Lebensüberdruss"geendeten   während des Gehens
      gross
/Lieblingsonkel geerbt/und immer geliebt haben,wir/erinnerten uns/nicht an
einen so tiefen Schnee und an einen so kalten Nachmittag,der schliesslich
                                       geworden
der kälteste Heilige Abend in diesem Jahrhundert/war,so die Statistik.

Schermaier eingeheizt etc.

er ist der Schriftsteller,ich bin der Internist etc.

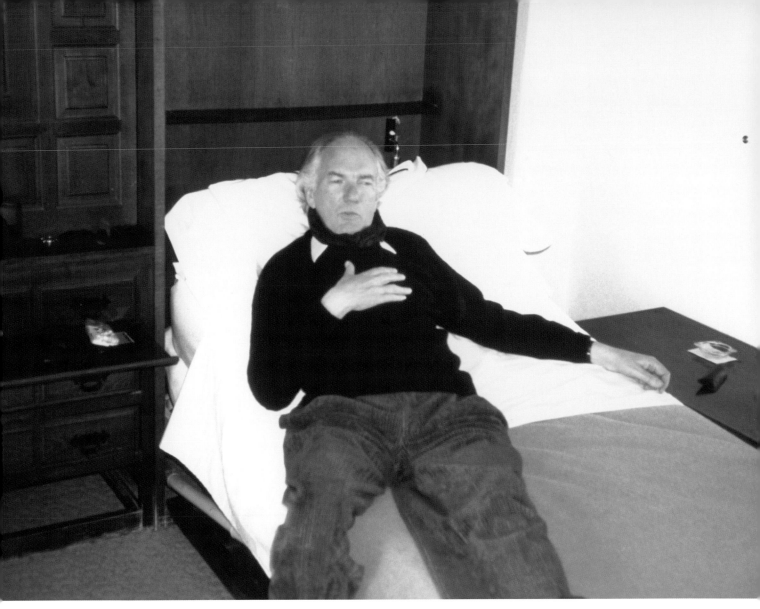

Thomas Bernhard, Spain (Torremolinos), late 1988

Neufundland/Newfoundland, typed manuscript

Opening sentence and draft for a final novel that was never written

Romanende

...und starb neunundfünfzigjährig in Neufundland.
ENDE.

Thomas Bernhard, Spain (Torremolinos), late 1988

Neufundland/Newfoundland, typed manuscript. Final sentence of a work not completed

Thomas Bernhard: Biography

1931   born on 9th Feb. in Heerlen (Netherlands), the illegitimate son of Herta Bernhard, daughter of the author, Johannes Freumbichler. Bernhard never meets his father Alois Zuckerstätter.

1931-35 lives with mother and her parents in Vienna; difficult economic situation, close relationship to grandfather on his mother's side.

1935   moves to Seekirchen am Wallersee (Province of Salzburg) with mother and grandparents.

1938   the family moves to Traunstein (Bavaria); Bernhard's mother and her husband, Emil Fabjan, have two more children: Peter (born in 1938) and Susanne (born in 1940).

1943   NS home for schoolchildren, grammar school; in the following years he has, among other subjects, violin and singing lessons.

1945   Johanneum (Catholic Home for schoolchildren).

1946   whole family moves to Salzburg (Radetzky-Str. 10).

1947   leaves grammar school prematurely, apprenticeship as shop assistant (Salzburg/Scherzhauserfeldsiedlung).

1949-51 as a result of TB several stays in hospital, sanatoriums and nursing homes (among others in the sanatorium for consumptives at Grafenhof near St.Veit/Pongau, Salzburg).

1949   death of grandfather.

1950   meets Hedwig Stavianicek – his ›Lebensmensch‹; death of mother.

1952-55 freelance work for the Salzburg ›Demokratisches Volksblatt‹, reports on court cases, reviews books, plays and films, first literary publications: poems, narratives.

1955   travels to Yugoslavia for the first time (with Hedwig Stavianicek).

1955-57 attends ›Mozarteum‹ academy of music and performing arts in Salzburg: music lessons, studies acting and directing.

1956   travels to Venice for the first time (with Hedwig Stavianicek).

1957-60 friendship with the composer Gerhard Lampersberg; long visits to his Tonhof in Maria Saal (Carinthia).

1957   first volume of poems: *Auf der Erde und in der Hölle*.

1958   *In hora mortis*, *Unter dem Eisen des Mondes* (vols. of poetry).

1959   *die rosen der einöde. fünf sätze für ballett, stimmen und orchester.*

1960   performance of the short opera *Köpfe* and some short plays in the theatre at Tonhof; travels to Italy for the first time (Rome, Sicily etc., with Hedwig Stavianicek), short stay in England (London).

1963   literary breakthrough with the novel *Frost/ Frost* (published by Insel, consequently most of his books are published by Suhrkamp of Frankfurt, under Siegfried Unseld); travels to Poland for the first time.

1964   *Amras*, the Julius Campe Prize.

1965   the Bremen Prize for Literature; buys farmhouse in Obernathal near Ohlsdorf (Upper Austria; which was arranged by the property dealer Karl Ignaz Hennetmair), long-term renovation of building, later buys two more houses at Reindmühl and Ottnang, in the meantime frequent stays in Vienna (at Hedwig Stavianicek's apartment in Obkirchergasse in Döbling) and journeys, especially to the Mediterranean (Yugoslavia etc.) where

some of his works originate;
travels to Italy (Rome etc.).

1967 *Verstörung/Gargoyles, Prosa*, has operation at pulmonary hospital of the City of Vienna on the Baumgartner Höhe.

1968 *Ungenach*; Kleiner Österreichischer Staatspreis (Austrian State Prize): caused stir at award ceremony; Anton Wildgans Prize.

1969 *Watten, Ereignisse* (written in 1957), *An der Baumgrenze/At the Timberline*.

1970 *Das Kalkwerk/The Lime Works, Ein Fest für Boris/A Party for Boris* (performed for the first time in Hamburg, directed by Claus Peymann who also produced most of his other plays), TV film *Drei Tage* (directed by Ferry Radax).

1971 *Gehen, Midland in Stilfs, Der Italiener* (filmed by Ferry Radax); gives readings during a tour through Italy and Yugoslavia.

1972 *Der Ignorant und der Wahnsinnige* (first performed at the Salzburg Festival); the Franz Theodor Csokor Prize, the Adolf Grimme Prize, the Grillparzer Prize.

1974 *Die Jagdgesellschaft* (first performed at Vienna Burgtheater), *Die Macht der Gewohnheit/The Force of Habit* (Salzburg Festival), *Der Kulterer* (filmed by Vojtech Jasny).

1975 *Die Ursache/An Indication of the Cause* (first of five vols. of autobiography, all published by Salzburg Residenz under Wolfgang Schaffler; libel action brought by local priest Franz Wesenauer), *Korrektur/Correction, Der Präsident/The President*; travels to Portugal for the first time.

1976 *Der Keller/The Cellar, Die Berühmten*.

1977 *Minetti*; travels extensively: to Italy (Rome, Sicily etc.), Iran, Egypt, and Israel.

1978 *Der Atem/Breath, Ja/Yes, Der Stimmenimitator/The Voice Impersonator, Immanuel Kant*; travels to Majorca for the first time.

1979 *Der Weltverbesserer, Vor dem Ruhestand/ Eve of Retirement*, withdrawal from the Deutsche Akademie für Sprache und Dichtung (German Academy of Language and Poetry).

1980 *Die Billigesser/The Cheap-Eaters*

1981 *Die Kälte/In the Cold, Über allen Gipfeln ist Ruh, Am Ziel, Ave Vergil* (vol. of poetry written towards the end of the 1950s); travels to Turkey.

1982 *Ein Kind/A Child, Beton/Concrete, Wittgensteins Neffe/Wittgenstein's Nephew*, Premio Prato.

1983 *Der Untergeher/The Loser, Der Schein trügt/ Appearances are Deceiving*, Premio Mondello; travels to Spain for the first time.

1984 death of Hedwig Stavianicek. *Holzfällen/Woodcutters* or *Cutting Timber* (temporary confiscation of the novel on Gerhard Lampersberg's instructions); *Der Theatermacher/Histrionics, Ritter, Dene, Voss/Ritter, Dene, Voss*.

1985 *Alte Meister/Old Masters*.

1986 *Auslöschung/Extinction, Einfach kompliziert*.

1987 *Elisabeth II*.

1988 *Heldenplatz/Heldenplatz* (much public discussion of Bernhard's play about the ›Bedenk-Jahr‹, the ›year of reflection‹: 50 years annexation of Austria by Nazi Germany); Prix Medicis; travels to Spain for the last time (Torremolinos).

1989 dies on 12th Feb. in Gmunden (Upper Austria) after many years of serious illness; buried beside Hedwig Stavianicek in Grinzing Cemetery in Vienna.

Bernhard's works are mentioned under their German and English titles if they have already been translated; texts that were not available in English translations are only given under their German titles.

His journeys are recorded as they are mentioned in Hedwig Stavianicek's notes.

Hedwig Stavianicek

1894-1984

I believe there are decisive people for everyone. I have had two in my life. My grandfather on my mother's side and then someone I met a year before my mother's death. That was a relationship that lasted more than 35 years. That was the person to whom everything that concerned me was related, who taught me everything. [...] If I was alone, no matter where, I always knew that this person would protect me, support me, even control me.

Thomas Bernhard in conversation with Asta Scheib

Hedwig Stavianicek,
Wagrain 1951

Hedwig Stavianicek and
Thomas Bernhard,
Dienten/Hochkönig
1958

Thomas Bernhard and Hedwig Stavianicek: Fact and Fiction

Manfred Mittermayer

> Right from the start, people thirst quite naturally for all the love and attention the world has to offer. When deprived of them, I'll say it a hundred times over, one feels cold and sees and hears nothing. It's a rather harsh reality. But it's unavoidable.
>
> Thomas Bernhard in conversation with Asta Scheib

1.

When Thomas Bernhard's narrative *Wittgensteins Neffe/Wittgenstein's Nephew* appeared in 1982, the author did more than honour the memory of his friend, Paul Wittgenstein (1907-1979), the nephew of the philosopher, Ludwig Wittgenstein. Bernhard also presented the most important person in his second half of life to his readers. The book begins with an account of the author's stay at Baumgartner Höhe Hospital in Vienna (which actually took place from 13 June until 4 September 1967). Bernhard wrote that he knew he had not only his friend Paul Wittgenstein close to him but also the one person he had not been able to live without for years. She was Hedwig Stavianicek, his companion and confidant of many decades. ›I had my *life person* in Vienna, the key person in my life after my grandfather's death, my life's companion, to whom, from the moment she turned up at my side over thirty years ago, I owed not only a great deal, to be perfectly frank, more or less everything‹ (WN 19). It is not coincidental that Bernhard introduced Stavianicek, whom he had met during a stay at the Grafenhof Tuberculosis Sanatorium (near St. Veit/Pongau in Salzburg Province), at his sickbed – like his grandmother Anna Bernhard, Hedwig Stavianicek had really studied nursing in her earlier years:

Hedwig Stavianicek with
one of her brothers

This woman, to me in every respect an exemplary, clever woman, who has never let me down for a single vital moment, from whom over the past thirty years I have learned practically everything or at least learned to understand practically everything, and from whom to this day I am learning things that matter or at least always learning to understand, then visited me almost every day and sat by my bedside.

(Ibid.)

On another occasion, both Paul Wittgenstein and Hedwig Stavianicek stand by Bernhard in the face of an uncomprehending and hostile society. The author describes the first spectacular scandal of his literary career, when he received the ›Austrian State Prize for Literature‹. In his acceptance speech, Bernhard uttered one of his most famous statements: ›Everything is ridiculous when one thinks about death.‹ According to Bernhard, the Minister of Education and all of the invited guests were so outraged by the comment that they stormed out of the hall, leaving Bernhard totally alone on stage. Even though eyewitnesses later recount that the incident was not quite as extreme as Bernhard remembers, the battle lines, nonetheless, had been drawn for the rest of his life: Bernhard, the artist, on one side and society-at-large on the other.

No one stood by me and my life person. Each of them stormed out of the hall, past the buffet set up for them, after the minister, and down the stairs — everyone except Paul. He was the only one who stayed behind with me and my *life's companion*, my life person, who was simultaneously horrified and amused by the incident.

(WN 84f.)

2.

Those who would like to have an understanding of the Bernhard-Stavianicek relationship can get some information from the recollections of Bernhard's contemporaries. In the book *Zeugenfreundschaft* (1999), Rudolf Brändle details the friendship between our young artist and this widow of a prominent Viennese official. (Brändle, by the way, is the *Kapellmeisterfreund* [choral director's friend] in Bernhard's autobiographical *Die Kälte/In the Cold*, 1981.) Brändle writes:

Hede Stavianicek was certainly not a wealthy woman, but she was not poor either. As the widow of a department head for the Ministry of Health, she received a small pension, which could support an entire family. I assume that she paid his small tuition bills, the rent for his room on Freumbichlerweg (!) in Parsch, and his other expenses. Although Thomas already had given up his career in music, he took voice lessons as a favour to her. His field of studies was theatre. Here, he acquired the tools necessary for becoming a playwright.

(Brändle 1999, 100.)

During the 1950s, Thomas Bernhard did live, as mentioned above, in a house at Johannes-Freumbichler-Weg 26, a street named after his grandfather. However, on 29 August 1957, he registered his address with the authorities as Obkirchergasse 3, 1190 Vienna – the home of Hedwig Stavianicek. From then on, he was a regular guest of Stavianicek's. In an interview with journalist Andre Müller, Bernhard describes his dependence upon Stavianicek:

I lived off my aunt for practically 15 years. She gave me a certain amount of pocket money every day. I believe it was about 10 Schillings back then. I spent seven fifty at a welfare kitchen in Vienna and two fifty at a local coffee house. That was enough. In the evening, I'd go wherever there were people and where there was something to eat and drink. Then, I'd go home around three in the morning.

(Müller 1992, 51)

Bernhard's readers may recognize the welfare kitchen he is talking about in his volume of prose entitled *Die Billigesser/The Cheap-Eaters*, published in 1980. Koller, the protagonist, is a loner and an intellectual. He falls upon hard times and finds himself at the kitchen and in the company of the so-called ›cheap-eaters‹, with whom he eats ›for many years on weekdays, that is from Mondays to Fridays, [...] cheaply at the Vienna Public Kitchen, at the so-called VPK, more particularly at the VPK in Döblinger Hauptstrasse‹ (CE 2).

However, unlike Koller, who dies before achieving his ambitions, Bernhard enjoyed success in the 1960s, partly as a result of Hedwig Stavianicek's support. After her death, Bernhard stressed, not only in *Wittgenstein's Nephew* but also in a conversation with Asta Scheib, Stavianicek's contributions to his literary success:

She was happy when she realised I was able to work [...] I never had a better critic than her [...] I only ever received strong, positive criticism from this woman, which was useful to me. She recognised me for who I am, with all my faults.

(Dreissinger 1992, 151)

One should keep in mind that her support was not purely intellectual, as Bernhard suggests. It was also emotional. She reassured him that he was not alone. Stavianicek provided, in many ways, the stability he had not had growing up. Bernhard grew up without a father and lost his beloved and respected grandfather in

Hedwig Stavianicek in nurse's uniform, 1915

1949. Moreover, his mother died in 1950 – the same year he met Hedwig Stavianicek. She was dependable and gave him a sense of direction. Bernhard once commented, ›I always knew that this person would be totally there for me when times were tough. All I needed to do was think about her, I didn't even need to look for her, and everything would be fine.‹ (Ibid.) Additionally, Bernhard said, ›On the one hand, she was for me a restraining force, a disciplinary force. And on the other, she opened up the world to me.‹ (Ibid., 140).

His fellow student at the Mozarteum, pianist Ingrid Bülau, confirmed this. She said that Stavianicek was Bernhard's ›most serious and deepest relationship‹. Stavianicek was ›exceptionally vigorous, clever, cultivated and very well-educated. She also made sure that he became disciplined and didn't just write anyhow, but worked hard and with discipline at shaping his whole work. All this was to her credit‹ (Fleischmann 1992, 34).

3.

Additional insights into the Bernhard-Stravianicek relationship can be gained by reading the numerous cards and letters they sent each other. A small selection of Stavianicek's letters

Hedwig Stavianicek

and self-discipline; now he is writing the short novel and how good it would be to have regular contact in singing, as he promised me! Always wanting to go somewhere else, isn't that running away from yourself? and from the unanswered questions in our souls? But it's no good, you can't run away from yourself, ›fighting against his life that lies here before us, our heritage and land that we can cultivate or neglect‹.

In that same year, Bernhard expresses the desire to find a ›real job‹: ›In an undisciplined lifestyle, that is, in the feeling of absolute freedom, lies a great danger. I shall seek with all my ability to find something.‹ On another occasion in 1955, he writes that, in his opinion, a person never escapes from ›vacillations‹. However, he also wonders whether, ›it would be dreadful, living life consistently every day.‹

can be seen in this exhibition. Bernhard's letters, however, are currently not available to the public. In this context I would like to thank Ms. Susanne Kuhn, Bernhard's sister, for providing the quotes in this essay (with the permission of Bernhard's brother and heir Dr. Peter Fabjan). Ms. Kuhn developed the concept of an exhibition on Hedwig Stavianicek in Bernhard's home in Ohlsdorf in 1996; much of that exhibition could be incorporated into our presentation in Vienna.

If anything, Stavianicek's letters demonstrate her desire to have a positive influence on Bernhard. His indecisiveness around his identity as an artist keep re-surfacing. Consequently, Stavianicek writes to him in 1955 and complains:

Wednesday, Thomas, my child, how he worries me with today's mad and fearful card! Is that the way the March winds shake him up? Where is the joyful, confident mood of late? I am wrestling to keep my own spiritual and physical equilibrium and he should thank God that he is healthy, be content with what he has and look forward to the good things the summer will bring, surely something wonderful and unexpected. A little patience

According to their correspondence they felt a mutual awkwardness around each other. Neither one seemed able to understand the nature of their relationship. For example, Stavianicek's letters demonstrate a problem she had with just how she should address this friend many years her junior. Clearly, she has trouble finding an appropriate salutation for him. At first, she refers to him as ›child‹; then, she uses ›he‹ as in the example above. It has less to do with condescension and more to do with an attempt at maintaining an appropriate distance and objectivity. She tries using ›Du‹, the familiar form of ›you‹ in German, and, then, reverts back to ›Sie‹, a more distant and polite form of address. It takes her fifteen years before she uses the obvious ›Dear Thomas‹, in a letter dated 4 June 1965. Hedwig Stavianicek gradually came to accept that he was not her willingly adopted son, but rather ›a highly individualized ego‹, whom she would have to learn to respect. ›I believe that we have both made the mistake of not imagining what it must be really like for the other, to affirm his qualities and allow him to become as he desires.‹ (Letter dated 28 September 1956)

166

Bernhard also struggles to understand what she means to him. In many of his letters, he reflects upon what role she plays in his life. ›The most beautiful time in life has passed,‹ he complains in 1955. ›I can never be a child again, never.‹ In the same year, he asks, ›Who do I still have here? You and my grandmother, who can give me very little because so many hungry hearts hang on her.‹ In 1957 he writes, ›What would I have done had it not been for Hede these past few years when I left the sinking ship of my family. My family has sunk and cannot be brought back!‹ By 1955, Bernhard confers upon his new life person ›the reverence, which had previously been reserved for my mother.‹ And in 1962, he repeats once again his assessment of their relationship which given the difference in their ages is self-evident: ›You are the dearest person to me. How can I say it any other way? My mother? Yes! Isn't that so?‹

Nevertheless, the following comment discloses another problem in his relationship with the ever-dependable and revered companion, which must have been eating away at the young man's self-esteem. In a letter penned in 1956, he writes, ›I confirm receipt of 300 Schillings from Hede, for which I am grateful a thousand times over. Just like a poor dog should be. Thanks !!!‹ Furthermore, Stavianicek's notebooks document Bernhard's financial dependence upon her. In detail, this frugal woman recorded each of her financial transactions, including money given or lent to him. For example, there are pages after pages of trivial entries such as: ›Thomas paper 13.10 [Schillings]‹, ›Thomas soap 9.50‹, ›Thomas, bread, 23.20‹, ›Thomas tailor 138.50‹ and even ›Thomas extra 20‹.

As mentioned, their relationship was more than just intellectually or financially supportive. It was also nurturing. Stavianicek expresses pleasure in her protege's first literary success, as if it were her own. She writes, on 30 November 1956, ›the publication of His [your]

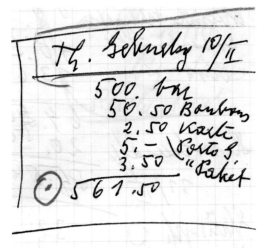

Entries in one of Hedwig Stavianicek's notebooks

first volume of poetry gives me such pleasure and His [your] ›I've done it‹ is the best present He [you] could give me.‹ She encourages him to keep writing. ›Even if dark and empty days will return, days of not-being-able, the certainty of »nothing can happen to me« will never leave Him [you], for that means He has recognized His true vocation and wants to go through with it and endure it.‹ However, once Bernhard begins enjoying greater literary acclaim in the 1960s, she is bewildered by his increasingly more radical perspectives. On 21 January 1966 she writes,

Both of your letters made me happy to know that you can work and disturbed me that you can be so rejecting and hostile towards friends and other people. Why not leave them as they are? Accept them for not being able to be different. Distance himself and preserve his own self without having to dirty himself with such angry feelings.

Finally, on 20 February 1966, she admits to being irritated by Bernhard's behaviour. To her, he has become ›difficult‹:

You are a difficult fellow, a difficult poet, you don't make life and reading easy for me and your readers, ›a great talent and talented people‹ can afford to make life pleasant for themselves and others, whereas a genious is invariably involved in battles in which he injures himself and others.

Hedwig Stavianicek and Thomas Bernhard, Nathal/Ohlsdorf, late 1960's

What a ›great genius‹ you must be as far as ›hurting your nearest‹ is concerned.‹

Nevertheless, Stavianicek does not stop supporting Bernhard and his work. To her mind, his first drama *Ein Fest für Boris/A Party for Boris* (1970) expresses ›what a great man says to his public and his audience: One must disturb them. Leave them perturbed and astonished.‹ And in a letter from 22 February 1969 she attempts to connect his secluded lifestyle with her deeply religious understanding of life:

--today there is yellowish-grey fog, drizzle, how well and safe I am in my lovely, warm apartment [...] You must feel really well and happy in your own property that you have acquired for yourself, without any company to disturb you! Mind you, ›being alone‹ doesn't mean being without any human contact, one is and always feels alone, only at the moment of giving, of giving yourself, of being able to help, is it all just forgetting ›Ich-alleinsein‹ [I-being-alone] or at the moment of the close feeling and recognition of ›being one‹ with God, the Creator (non-religious), just like the great mystics or truly religious people. Not feeling close or one with God is the only true sin of mankind (that I acknowledge)-

Gradually, Hedwig Stavianicek acquires an appreciation of Bernhard's art and lifestyle. Just as she was the first to open his eyes to the world, she realizes that, through him, her own view of the world has changed. In her

own environment, she encounters ›over and over again prejudices and rigid points of view‹ and the refusal ›to think beyond one's own experiences and daily routine‹ (letter dated 3 February 1970). Additionally, she writes in her letters that she feels lucky that she can still be with him to enjoy his successes even though her letters complain of old age, its aches and pains.

In the last years of her life, Hedwig Stavianicek stops writing letters. Instead, she sends postcards with short messages. In Bernhard's postcards from his travels without her, he writes about places that they once had visited together or that she would have enjoyed and that she is no longer able to come along.

4.

As we have seen in the first part of the catalogue (on Johannes Freumbichler, Bernhard's grandfather), the subject matter for Bernhard's writings comes directly from his personal experiences and encounters with people important to him. Real world events enter the realm of his imagination and, eventually, take on a meaning of their own within the framework of his artistic considerations. Nevertheless, parallels do exist between real life and fiction, and Freumbichler is a good example of this.

On one level, Bernhard attempts to come to terms with himself and the contradictions of his personality. In his books of fiction, Bernhard reveals insightful self-reflection on topics and problems. The goal of this internal struggle may have been to seek some sort of understanding of the darker side of his personality and to develop his own character as an artist.

As his work progressed, it developed a sign of success – a sense of irony. Additionally, in the context of the development of his five-volume autobiography, explicitly fictional texts began to allude to real life experiences. Since the mid-

1970s and the release of *Die Ursache/An Indication of the Cause* (1975), reality and fiction started to merge together. One needs only to think about *Ja/Yes* (1978) where the protagonist, just like Bernhard, is renovating a house and is friends with a real estate agent named Moritz – who is clearly modelled after a real person, Karl Ignaz Hennetmair.

Just as there is an analogy between Hennetmair and Moritz, Bernhard's last work of prose, *Alte Meister/Old Masters* (1985; *Auslöschung/Extinction*, 1986, had been written for the most part in 1981/82), can be interpreted as a literary requiem dedicated to Hedwig Stavianicek. The main character, Reger, a music critic, grieves the devastating loss of his wife and struggles to maintain control over his life. In lengthier passages, Bernhard demonstrates and reflects upon the emotional difficulties a man faces while coping with the loss of his most precious loved-one. After the death of his wife, Reger first thinks about moving out of his home because everything there reminds him of his wife: ›[...] no matter where I look, she is always standing here, sitting there, coming towards me from this room or that, it is terrible even though, at the same time it is heart-rending‹ (OM 131). However, he does not have the energy for that. Additionally, he constantly is being tortured by guilt: now that his wife is dead, it is too late for explanations or apologies.

The things we inflicted on that one beloved person, Reger said, the thousands and hundreds of thousands of pains we inflicted on this one person whom we loved more than anyone else, the torments we inflicted on that person, and yet we loved them more than anyone else, Reger said. When that person whom we loved more than anyone else is dead they leave us with a terribly guilty conscience, Reger said [...]

(OM 143).

With the help of a rigid daily routine, Reger gradually recovers from grieving. On alternating days, he goes either to the Vienna Mu-

seum of Fine Arts or to the cemetery to his wife's grave. ›I have made it a habit to visit my wife's grave every other day, the grave which one day will also be my own, Reger said‹ (OM 133). Here, fact and fiction overlap. By now, Bernhard knew that he was terminally ill and, probably within a few short years, would be lying in Hedwig Stavianicek's grave. Analogous to Bernhard's life is the way Reger describes the beginning of his relationship with his wife. After his parents' death, he met his wife – ›at the moment when I did no longer know which way to turn.‹ Reger adds, ›My wife saved me; I had always been afraid of the female sex and *in fact* in a manner of speaking *hated women body and soul* and yet, he said, his wife saved him‹ (OM 97). Inevitably, one makes an association with the image of women in Bernhard's earlier books. They oppose everything that is *männlich-geistig* [of male intellect]. Also, one thinks of the eruption of hate from characters such as Strauch in *Frost* (1963), Konrad in *Das Kalkwerk/The Lime Works* (1970) or Roithamer in *Korrektur/Correction* (1975). Each one bears witness simultaneously to an ingrained fear of women. Do such passages not allude, ironically, to the author's own personal development?

However, *Old Masters* is not the first work in which Bernhard draws upon the death of a loved-one as his subject matter. Having lost his maternal grandfather and then his mother at critical times in his life, it is certainly no coincidence that the author creates plots which seem to be reactions to these circumstances. Many of his protagonists attempt to keep hold of their loved ones forever. In order to make their companions adapt to their own selfish needs these characters create relationships which terrorize their loved ones. At least three of them come to mind: there is Konrad in *The Lime Works*, who (after a year-long relationship with his wife and half-sister) confesses that there is not a single person in the entire world who is absolutely right for him; Roithamer in *Correction*, who constructs a cone as a kind of home-cum-prison for his beloved sister; and, most of all, Wertheimer in *Der Untergeher/The Loser* (1983). Wertheimer, whose sister marries just to escape his oppressive demands, intentionally kills himself in front of her house so that she will feel forever guilty for having abandoned him.

Similarly, Karl, one of the two brothers in *Der Schein trügt/Appearances are Deceiving* (1983), attempts to change his common law wife but now must cope her with death:

We take a woman for eternity
commit ourselves to her for ever
and she leaves us at the most inconvenient
moment
(Sch 12f.)

Just prior to the publishing of this play, the actress Edith Heerdegen had died. (She had played the part of the wife in Der *Weltverbesserer/The Reformer of the World*, 1979.) Bernhard honoured her by weaving her death into his play. But apart from that, he appears to have acted out an event that he would have to cope with in the immediate future: Hedwig Stavianicek's death. On the occasion of a visit from Bernhard and Stavianicek in 1980, the Austrian author Hilde Spiel wrote, ›Thomas seems to want to learn from me how to cope with the death of someone close to him.‹ (Huguet [1995], 464) Spiel had just lost her husband, Hans Flesch-Brunningen, a contemporary of Stavianicek.

›I miss her,‹ Karl admits. ›After all for thirty years / we shared everything‹ (Sch 45). He would spend his evenings ›sitting there / thinking about her / motionlessly.‹ Then, he would go to bed and would not be able to sleep: ›I think only of Mathilde‹ (Sch 79). He talked incessantly about her wonderful fish dinners and how badly she played the piano, the Mozart sonata that she would play daily in the most horrible way. Thus, we see another side Karl's relationship to Mathilde, who showed a com-

plete lack of artistic talent despite Karl's efforts to educate her to his satisfaction. ›We have to accept one terrible trait / when we have a partner,‹ Karl mentions at the beginning of the piece (Sch 19). In another place, he states even more clearly:

When we think back
it is frightening
what we have had to put up with all our lives
(Sch 65)

In his narrative *Beton/Concrete* (1982), Bernhard describes another highly ambivalent relationship between a man and a woman of great importance to him. Rudolf, the book's main character, is a writer who lives in a secluded house which sounds very similar to Bernhard's farmhouse in Ohlsdorf. (In the chapter regarding Johannes Freumbichler, in this catalogue, we have already seen many other striking similarities between Bernhard and Rudolf.) The book begins with the protagonist trying to recover from his sister's visit. He blames her for his difficulty in writing:

How many essays have I begun, only to burn them because my sister turned up, only to throw them in the stove the moment she's appeared! No one is so fond of saying, *I'm not disturbing you, am I?* That's rich coming from someone who's always disturbed people and always will, whose sole mission in life seems to be to disturb, to disturb anything and everything and so destroy it and finally annihilate it, constantly to annihilate what to me is the most important thing in the world — a product of the mind.

(Co 6)

Almost immediately, we are reminded of Konrad's ominous dream in *The Lime Works* in which he watches his wife (who is also his half-sister) burn his research study — a book which he has worked on for many years. Shortly thereafter, Konrad kills her because he believes that she was his greatest enemy when it came to intellectual work. Thus *Concrete* presents a less extreme version of one of

Bernhard's favourite subjects. Additionally, however, we may associate Brändle's account of Bernhard's difficulties with Hedwig Stavianicek. In Stavianicek's home at Obkirchergasse, Bernhard required absolute privacy in order to write. Yet, Stavianicek who was ›used to checking on her company, just would not accept that he needed privacy in order to write,‹ Brändle wrote in *Zeugenfreundschaft*. ›Just as he would be getting into the flow of writing, she would look in and inquire how things were going. Or, at least, that's what he often said she did‹ (Brändle 1999, 105).

We find a second personality trait which Rudolf ascribes to his sister and which also sounds very much like Hedwig Stavianicek: ›She's a business woman. Even as a very small child she was that way inclined, towards the persecution of the intellect and the closely concomitant pursuit of money.‹ (Co 8). Anyone who has seen Stavianicek's ledgers with column after column of entries understands that Bernhard is taking aim at his life person. Rudolf continues, ›She's always been the realistic one just as I've always been the imaginative one. *I love you because you're so imaginative*, she often says, but there's more disdain than admiration in this remark.‹ (Co 34) One must ask if Bernhard, in *Concrete*, is attempting to come to terms with certain irritating aspects of his life friend by projecting them onto Rudolf's sister. Thus he does not disturb his perfect image of Stavianicek as his personal saviour.

Nonetheless, just as Rudolf describes her, his sister proves to be an angry and argumentative persecutor of intellectuals right from the very beginning of the book. ›Women surface, attach themselves to a man, and then ruin him,‹ Rudolf claims referring to his sister. Nevertheless, a few lines later, he confesses that he had invited her to visit. ›It's true that I wired for her help: she didn't come to Peiskam uninvited.‹ (Co 22) So Rudolf's sister is the

Hedwig Stavianicek and Thomas Bernhard, Vienna 1982

woman he calls when he is in great difficulties. But apart from that, she criticizes her brother's lifestyle – and at the same time the way the author himself leads his life:

You despise everything, she said, everything in the world. Everything that gives me pleasure you despise. And above all you despise yourself. *You accuse everybody of every possible crime. That's your misfortune*. That's what she said, and at first I didn't appreciate the full enormity of it. Only now do I realize that she'd hit the nail on the head. I enjoy life, she said, though I have my sufferings too. Everybody suffers, my dear little brother, but you despise life. That's your misfortune, that's why you're ill, that's why you´re dying. And you soon will die if you don't change, she said [...] My sister the clairvoyant – absurd!

(Co 20f.)

Talking about Hedwig Stavianicek, Franz-Josef Altenburg, who was a mutual friend of theirs, commented, ›She had intelligence and a sharp tongue. She could be extremely caustic. She visited us once and said, »Take a look! This is living – not like at your place!«‹ (Fialik 1991, 145) Rudolf reacts to his sister with selfaccusations. ›I imagine I needed no one, and this is what I still imagine to this day. [...] But naturally we do need someone, otherwise we inevitably become what I have become: tiresome, unbearable, sick – impossible, in the profoundest sense of the word‹ (Co 27). And he delivers one of the most striking example of am-

Hedwig Stavianicek and Thomas Bernhard, Nathal/Ohlsdorf 1980

bivalence to be found in Bernhard's works, which are in fact rich with contradictions:

I always believed that I could get on with my intellectual work if only I were completely alone, with no one else around. This proved to be mistaken, but it is equally mistaken to say that we actually need someone. We need someone for our work, we also need no one. Sometimes we need someone, sometimes no one, and some-times we need someone and no one. In the last few days I have once more become aware of this totally absurd fact [...].

(Co 27)

In Bernhard's *Concrete*, the writer Rudolf reflects upon his isolation and the many contradictions in his relationship with his sister, whom he needs more than anyone else, whose strength, however, causes him to feel inferior to her. ›The little brother is powerless in the face of such a radiant person, which is what she often calls herself. Every room is transformed when she enters it; wherever and whenever she appears, everything changes and becomes subordinate to her alone‹ (Co 42). As Rudolf allows himself to be saved from isolation by this person, he recognizes his own weaknesses even more. His sister actually succeeds in setting Rudolf free from his isolation, and finally he even believes that she has been planning from the very beginning the

trip to Palma de Mallorca which he undertakes at the end of the book. Incessantly, she needles him to leave the house. ›No one is as fond of travelling as you, yet you've been sitting around here for eighteen months and are dying. She said this quite calmly, like a doctor, as it now strikes me‹ (Co 86). Rudolf gives in and travels to Mallorca (which Bernhard visited several times during his later years). ›She achieved her goal. My big caring sister! At that moment I despised myself. Once more I was the weak one. Again and again I played my accustomed role, however much I rebelled against it‹ (Co 80).

As we have seen above, *Concrete* does not contain Bernhard's last word on the relationship between a man and his ›life person‹. Already before *Old Masters*, in the novel *Holzfällen/Woodcutters*, we find some lines that could be a reference to the author's bond with Hedwig Stavianicek (the book was published in 1984, the year Stavianicek died). It is a passage, however, that might also be understood as a commentary on Bernhard's reliance upon his grandfather. Through the narrator of the book, the author sets to words a most beautiful declaration of his love for older people:

During the course of my life I think I have become more interested in the old and the very old than in the young; more and more I have sought out the company of the old and the very old and spent more and more of my time with them, rather than with the young. After all, I knew about youth when I myself was young, but not about old age. Hence it was old age that interested me, not youth. *Get all you can out of the old*, I always told myself, and indeed I always derived the greatest benefit from following this precept; I have no hesitation in saying that I derived immense profit from it.

(Wo 175)

One year later came the literary farewell to the ›life person‹ who had since died. In *Old Masters* the music critic Reger is forced to see

172

the void left in his own life by the death of a loved one. Especially noteworthy is that Reger realizes that his wife was the single most important person in his life and that she profoundly influenced his appreciation of philosophy and art. ›I have always thought that it was music that meant everything to me,‹ Reger confesses, ›and at times that it was philosophy, or great or greatest of the very greatest writing, or altogether that it was simply art, but one of it, the whole of art or whatever, is nothing compared to that one beloved person‹ (OM 143). Bernhard's works are filled with *Geistesmenschen* [mind people], as the author calls them, intellectuals and artists, who consider a *Geistesprodukt* [a product of the mind] to be the highest thing one can achieve in life.

In his last novel, however, the protagonist questions the value of philosophy and art when he experiences the loss of the ›only person he loved‹:

When you have lost your closest human being everything seems empty to you, look wherever you like, everything is empty, and you look and look and you see that everything is *really empty*, and, what is more, for ever, Reger said. And you realize that it was not those great minds and not those old masters which kept you alive for decades but that it was this one single person whom you loved more than anyone else. And you stand alone in this realization and with this realization and there is nothing and no one to help you, Reger said.

(OM 144f.)

In this essay we did not especially indicate which of Bernhard's texts have actually been translated into English. A list of these translated texts can be found in Bernhard's biography, p. 158f. The other titles are loose translations of the German originals.

Quotations from Bernhard's texts were taken from the following translations:

CE   *The Cheap-Eaters*, trans. Ewald Osers. London, New York: Quartet 1990.
Co   *Concrete*, trans. David McLintock. London, New York: Quartet 1989.
OM   *Old Masters*, trans. Ewald Osers. London, New York: Quartet 1989.
Wo   *Woodcutters*, trans. David McLintock. New York: Knopf 1987.
WN   *Wittgenstein´s Nephew*, trans. Ewald Osers. London: Quartet 1986.

In all other cases the German versions were translated for this essay:

Sch   Thomas Bernhard: *Der Schein trügt*. Frankfurt am Main: Suhrkamp 1983.

Brändle, Rudolf: *Zeugenfreundschaft*. Salzburg, Vienna: Residenz 1999.
Dreissinger, Sepp (ed.): *Von einer Katastrophe in die andere. 13 Gespräche mit Thomas Bernhard*. Weitra: Bibliothek der Provinz 1992.
Fialik, Maria: *Der Charismatiker. Thomas Bernhard und die Freunde von einst*. Vienna: Böhlau 1992.
Fleischmann, Krista (ed.): *Thomas Bernhard – Eine Erinnerung. Interviews zur Person*. Vienna: Edition S 1992.
Huguet, Louis: *Chronologie. Johannes Freumbichler – Thomas Bernhard*. Weitra: Bibliothek der Provinz [1995].
Müller, André: *Im Gespräch mit Thomas Bernhard*. Weitra: Bibliothek der Provinz 1992.

Hedwig Hofbauer
with her parents

Hedwig Hofbauer with her four brothers on holiday in Neuhaus

HERTA
Frau Professor is going to take me along to Neuhaus

FRAU ZITTEL
She needs you there
I convinced her that she needs you [...]
In Neuhaus it's still really cold in March
we never went to Neuhaus in winter
but we have no choice
we have to go to Neuhaus
They were barely five years old
when they met in Neuhaus
It never works when people get married
who knew each other as children [...]
All I did in Neuhaus
was scrub floors day and night
I won't do that anymore   HERTA
no matter how often Frau Professor asks me to That's all he did
I did everything for Herr Professor
but not for her   FRAU ZITTEL
she only gives orders   But it was different

Heldenplatz

Announcing a private
drama production
(Hedwig Hofbauer being
one of the actors)

Hedwig Hofbauer

RITTER
The acting business
That's all that was left for us
nothing more
I never wanted a profession
and you

DENE
I don't know

RITTER
You had stage presence

DENE
Yes perhaps

RITTER
In comedies
and tragedies

DENE
Just because our uncle
was a theatre manager

RITTER
The daughters of Worringer the industrial tycoon
fled to their theatre manager uncle
because they were bored
had had enough of life
ended up in the Josefstadt theatre

Ritter, Dene, Voss

176

Hedwig Hofbauer

Hedwig Hofbauer

I still clearly remember a rendering of *Die letzten Tage der Menschheit* (*The Last Days of Mankind*) by Karl Kraus where she was so upset by the degrading way in which the Austrian officers were depicted that we had to turn it off. Her conservatism was in contrast to her behaviour as an emancipated woman. So as not to be considered old-fashioned she often talked of her youth, of riding astride the horse (as opposed to side-saddle) and of bathing naked in the Danube. She liked to think of herself as the black sheep of the family, of the Hofbauer tinned-fish-dynasty, originally from southern Bohemia.

Rudolf Brändle: *Zeugenfreundschaft*

Hedwig Hofbauer

Personal document at the Imperial and Royal
Military Hospital in Grinzing/Vienna

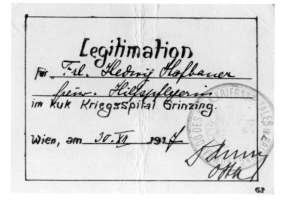

National Institute for Mothers' and Babies' Care in Vienna

178

Hedwig Hofbauer in nurse's uniform, 1915

I was never satisfied with my life. But I always felt
a great desire to be protected. I found this protec-
tion in my (female) friend. Somehow she always
got me to work. She was happy when she saw I
was doing something. That's why it was great.

Thomas Bernhard in conversation with Asta Scheib

Hedwig Stavianicek, Vienna/Ober-St. Veit 1951   Dr. Franz Stavianicek (1874-1944), Sorrent 1935

Marriage Certificate of Dr. Franz and Hedwig Stavianicek

Ministerialrat
Med. Dr. Franz Stavianicek

Bundesministerium für soziale Verwaltung

Dr. Stavianicek's visiting card

180

Hedwig Stavianicek

Hedwig Stavinanicek
and Thomas Bernhard,
St. Veit/Pongau 1953

We were usually alone with our music, only once, while Thomas was singing some pieces from Anna Magdalena Bach's Song Book, did two elderly ladies and a young girl come into the church. They listened in silence, and when the singing came to an end and both performers climbed down from the organ they came over to us and it turned out that they were old friends of Anna Janka's. They just could not believe that the beautiful and powerful voice belonged to that lanky young man. [...] It is rather a coincidence that this episode is briefly recorded in my pocket diary under 27th July 1950, because, as far as the time in Grafenhof is concerned, there are very few entries.

Rudolf Brändle: *Zeugenfreundschaft*

Hedwig Stavianicek on her earliest meetings
with Thomas Bernhard

Thomas Bernhard, St. Veit/Pongau 1953

Bernhard's address in one of Stavianicek's notebooks:
Salzburg, Freumbichler-Weg 26

Pocket calendar
with notes by
Hedwig Stavianicek

Water colour painting by Anna Janka

Anna Janka (1897-1973)
She studied at the Vienna School of Music, stayed on
and off at Grafenhof between 1940 and 1940, and
thereafter was the organist at the church of St. Veit/
Pongau (until 1970)

Anna Janka, a delicate, white-haired lady was a
trained musician. In her early years she was sent
as a patient to Grafenhof and spent the rest of her
life in St. Veit where she earned herself some extra
money as leader of the church choir. She lived in a
garret in the so-called Poor House, just a few steps
from the church, which was filled with rustic furni-
ture, a harmonium and souvenirs of all kinds. The
oil paintings and water-colours on the walls were
proof of the other talents of the person living there.
[...] Thomas had a special liking for the atmosphere
of the house, which reminded him of his childhood
in Traunstein.

Rudolf Brändle: *Zeugenfreundschaft*

I discussed my bad luck with my friend the organist. She was a Viennese, an artist, a graduate of
the Music Academy, and a professor. She had been
sent to Grafenhof during the war and as a result
had become a real victim of lung disease.
Afterwards she had stayed on in the village. From
now on she was my favourite companion, my new
teacher, the one person on whom I could rely. I
went to see her whenever I could.

In the Cold

Newspaper cutting (kept by
Hedwig Stavianicek): The
church of St. Veit/Pongau

SCHÖNE ERZDIÖZESE SALZBURG: Pfarrkirche von St. Veit (Blick vom
Altar zur Empore). Das vierschiffige Langhaus im gotischen Stil stammt aus
der zweiten Hälfte des 14. Jahrhunderts. Kirchenpatron ist der heilige Not-
helfer Vitus, der bekanntlich unter dem römischen Kaiser Diokletian (um 303)
den Märtyrertod starb. — St. Veit ist eine der ältesten Pfarren und gehörte
seinerzeit dem Salzburger Domkapitel.   Photo: Jeiter

Thomas Bernhard, St. Veit/Pongau 1956

Rudolf Brändle (b. 1922).
Studied music at the Mozarteum in Salzburg. Repetiteur,
accompanist, choral director and composer. Member of the
Vienna Volksoper company, 1958-1984.

Grafenhof TB sanatorium

I attached myself to a young man about ten years
older than myself – despite this difference in age
he was still very youthful – whom I first saw sitting
alone at the harmonium in the chapel, improvising
on a theme by Bach. He was a conductor by profession [...]. This was the start of a friendship that
has lasted until today, a friendship born of shared
suffering of ever there was one.

In the Cold

186

Thomas Bernhard, Rudolf Brändle's wife-to-be Tatjana, Mrs. Jung (an acquaintance), and Rudolf Brändle, at Erentrudisalpe/Salzburg 1953

Thomas Bernhard described how we met in his memoirs. [...] as far as chronological order is concerned there was a certain amount of poetic licence due to the form of the narrative. Thus Bernhard gives an account of how, after arriving at Grafenhof, he anxiously looked around for a fellow sufferer whom he could talk to, but he didn't find anyone, at least not during the first weeks. The following dates prove the contrary: Bernhard's arrival at Grafenhof on 27th July 1949 and my departure on 20th August 1949 means that we spent a total of 24 days together during our first stay there. Thomas must have already discovered me playing the organ in the chapel during the first days, and spoke to me immediately after this.

Rudolf Brändle: *Zeugenfreundschaft*

Thomas Bernhard,
Hedwig Stavianicek,
and Carla Kluge (an
acquaintance for many
years), Salzburg
(main station) 1954

188

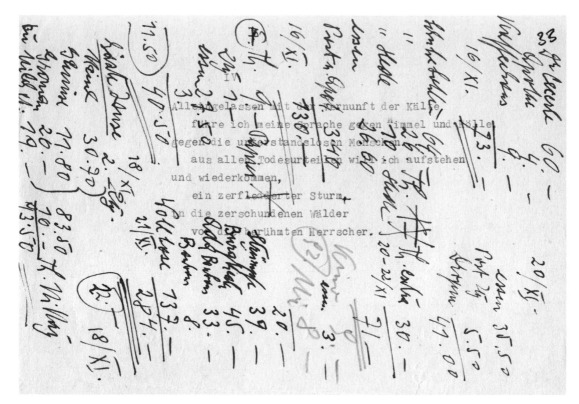

Typed copies of some of Bernhard's poems – used by Hedwig Stavianicek as a basis for her lists of numbers

Donauerhof in St. Veit/Pongau. For many years, the vacation home of Thomas Bernhard and Hedwig Stavianicek

Letter from Hedwig Stavianicek to Thomas Bernhard

Thomas Niklas, you cost me 8 Sch., telephone calls, two trips to the book-store!! till I got ›Wort in der Zeit‹, oh about the things we do in order to obtain the beautiful, immortal words of a young poet! Read several times, this new form of poetry has completely captivated me, Thomas, I'm so glad!

Hedwig Stavianicek and Thomas Bernhard, Dubrovnik 1962

Drafts by Thomas Bernhard written
on a Yugoslavian boat ticket

Trebinje (from Stavianicek´s extensive collection of postcards)

We went on journeys. I carried her heavy suitcases, but I got to know a lot. [...] Without stuffing me full, despite her being a devoted student of culture. It was all rather incidental. We went to Rome, to Split – yet it was always the inner journeys that one made.

Thomas Bernhard in conversation with Asta Scheib

Drafts by Thomas Bernhard
written on a Croatian newspaper

Hedwig Stavianicek, Mondsee 1969

Thomas Bernhard in the early 1960s

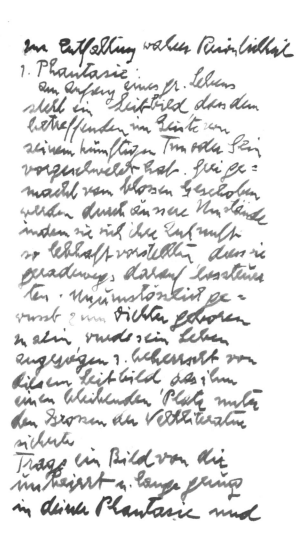

On The Development of True Personality
1. Imagination:
At the beginning of a great life there is guiding
image in that person's mind of what he will do or
be in the future. Freed from merely being pushed
through external circumstances by imagining their
future so vividly that they instantly start steering
towards it. Knowing incontrovertibly that he was
born to be a poet he took on this life and was
dominated by the guiding-image that would secure
him a permanent place among the great writers of
the world's literature.
Keep this unshaken image of yourself long enough
in your imagination and it will attract you magneti-
cally.
2. Courage. Really great personalities always have
that belief in themselves that gives them courage.
Belief in oneself has nothing to do with credulity. It
has an element of creativity: it's visionary strength
mixed with boldness.

Notes by Hedwig Stavianicek

Hedwig Stavianicek, Nathal/Ohlsdorf 1969

I was pleased and shocked about your letter – not the image of the captain in chaos, thinking, ordering, managing, but the over-emphasis of the ›Herrenmensch‹, the rejection, even contempt you feel for your neighbours, what bitter experiences you must have had with them once more!

Notes by Hedwig Stavianicek on Thomas Bernhard

193

Hedwig Stavianicek's pocket calendar
with notes regarding the first night of *A Party for Boris*

Invitation to the presentation of *Drei Tage/Three Days*
(by the film director, Ferry Radax) with notes
by Hedwig Stavianicek

Hedwig Stavianicek, Gmunden 1969

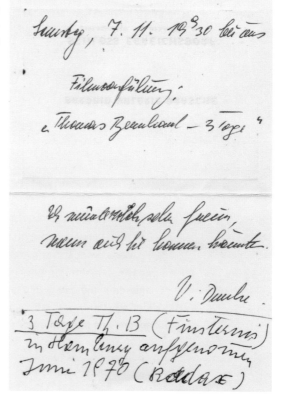

Thomas Bernhard during the production of *Three Days*, Hamburg 1970

In February, beginning of March 1968, driving a Puch Haflinger with four-wheel drive and chains, I went to his farm-house in Obernathal which was covered in snow. [...] I arrived after dark, the gate to the courtyard was open. There was a faint light. And who was looking sternly out of the window, without opening the door for me? ›Aunt‹. The atmosphere was frosty in every sense. [*Frost* is also the title of Bernhard's first novel!]

Ferry Radax in *Der Charismatiker*, Interviews with Maria Fialik

Hedwig Stavianicek,
Krucka
(one of Bernhard's
homes in Upper Austria)
1977

- I have never had such a close critical look, or felt so mentally stimulated by any of your books, partly agreeing, partly disagreeing, as with this one, it is fascinating, your thoughts entangle like creepers, poisonous, in the jungle of everyday life! and don't let you go – to me Konrad represents you yourself, who you are, what you are like, what you do – [...]
To me you are an example of making a pleasantly tolerable comedy out of the tragedy of human existence as it is known, instead of giving up voluntarily, or escaping into mental comfort!!
- or as Konrad thinks, mankind has tried the reverse [to make a tragedy out of their existential comedy]!!
- rationally it is an ever-recurring, constant comedy, emotionally, however, a tragedy!

Hedwig Stavianicek writing about the novel *Das Kalkwerk /
The Lime Works* to Thomas Bernhard, 27.9.1970

Hedwig Stavianicek, St. Veit/Pongau 1974

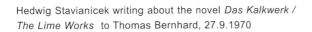

Siegfried Unseld and Hedwig Stavianicek, Salzburg 1974
(first night of *Die Macht der Gewohnheit/The Force of Habit*)

Notes by Hedwig Stavianicek
(e.g. from *The Force of Habit*: ›Life
consists in destroying questions.‹)

Hedwig Stavianicek, St. Veit/Pongau, mid-1970s

Hedwig Stavianicek and Thomas Bernhard, Krucka 1977

Notes in Hedwig Stavianicek's pocket calendar

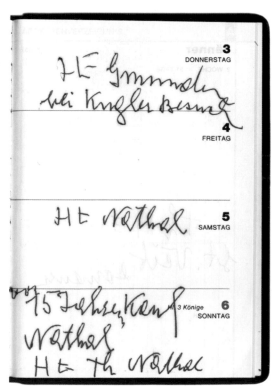

[...] I had my *life person* in Vienna, the key person in my life after my grandfather's death, my life's companion, to whom, from the moment she had turned up at my side over thirty years ago, I owed not only a great deal but, to be perfectly frank, more or less everything. Without her I would not be alive at all and I certainly would never be the person I am today, so crazy and so unhappy, but happy too as always.

Wittgenstein's Nephew

Dr. Peter Fabjan, Hedwig Stavianicek, and Thomas Bernhard, Krucka 1977

My mother died aged 46. That was in 1950. One year prior to that I met my life's companion. At first it was friendship and then it became a very strong bond with a much older person. Wherever I was in the world that was the focal point I actually took everything from. I always knew that that person would be there for me completely, if things got difficult.

Thomas Bernhard in conversation with Asta Scheib

Rudolf Brändle, Hedwig Stavianicek, and Thomas Bernhard,
Lovran 1980

Hedwig Stavianicek, Semmering
(Panhans Hotel) 1983

HERRENSTEIN
Semmering is a philosophical region
unlike the Salzkammergut
where dummies thrive
the second class and the third class
not like on Semmering the first class
You know Semmering as well as I do
Today it's no longer fashionable
to drive to Semmering
it's just for old people
that's why I go there

GUGGENHEIM
When we were children
we went every year to Semmering
to the Panhans
is it still there

HERRENSTEIN
Everything is there Guggenheim
but you wouldn't recognize a thing

Elisabeth II

Hedwig Stavianicek, Vienna/Obkirchergasse 1982

Thomas Bernhard's entry in Hedwig Stavianicek's last pocket calendar: ›Hede died at half past twelve in my arms‹

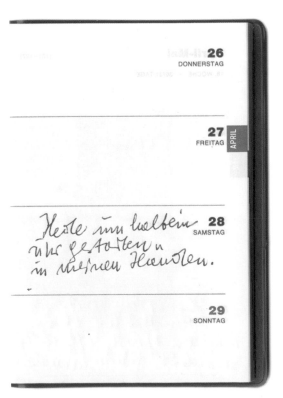

Of course we get used to a person over the decades and love them for decades and eventually love them more than anything else and cling to them and when we lose them it is truly as if we had lost *everything*. I have always thought that it was music that meant everything to me, and at times that it was philosophy, or great or greatest or the very greatest writing, or altogether that it was simply art, but none of it, the whole of art or whatever, is nothing compared to that one beloved person.

Old Masters

Hedwig Stavianicek,
Semmering 1982

Grave in Grinzing Cemetery

Mai   (128—134)   **10**
19. WOCHE · 31 TAGE   DONNERSTAG

7   **11**
MONTAG   FREITAG

8   **12**
DIENSTAG   SAMSTAG

9   **13**
MITTWOCH   SONNTAG

Thomas Bernhard's entry in Hedwig Stavianicek's last pocket calendar:
›H. buried in Grinzing Cemetery [...] where *I will also get into*‹

Hedwig Stavianicek: Biography

1894   birth of Hedwig Stavianicek (18.10) daughter of Franz and Maria Hofbauer (nee Weisskopf), an upper middle-class Viennese family. Father and mother come from Hutau (Bohemia) and Nikolsburg (Moravia) respectively. Four brothers.

1913   spends some time in Cambridge.

1916-17 serves as ›voluntary, unpaid auxiliary nurse‹ in Imperial and Royal Military Hospital in Grinzing/Vienna.

1919-20 trains and qualifies in infant welfare.

1928   marriage to Hermann Turnwald annulled after one year.

1933   marries Dr. Franz Maria Stavianicek (17.2), doctor of medicine and ministerial civil servant in the Department of Welfare.

1937   moves out of parents' villa, Weimarerstr. 89, to ›Haus am Steig‹, Grinzingerstr. 9.

1944   stays in TB sanatorium Grafenhof in St. Veit/Pongau. Dr. Franz Stavianicek dies, aged 70, in Vienna.

1950   meets Thomas Bernhard in the church of St. Veit.

1954   first correspondence between Hedwig Stavianicek and Thomas Bernhard.

1955   first joint trip abroad to Lovran (Croatia).

1957   moves into a three-roomed apartment in Döbling/Vienna, where she takes in the young Thomas Bernhard.

1965   Thomas Bernhard buys farmhouse in Nathal, Hedwig Stavianicek visits him regularly, often staying for weeks at a time in summer.

1967   pays for Thomas Bernhard's stay in the TB sanatorium ›Baumgartner Höhe‹ in Vienna. During the following years they experience the highs and lows of a poet's lot: Premieres, tributes, as well as numerous journeys abroad and in Austria. Hedwig Stavianicek is the focal point of Bernhard's life, his life becomes hers too, for nearly thirty years.
Health problems gradually start to keep Hedwig Stavianicek tied to her apartment more and more.

1982   Christmas: their last journey together to Panhans Hotel, Semmering.

1984   Hedwig Stavianicek dies in hospital on the ›Baumgartner Höhe‹ (28.4).
She is buried in her husband's grave in Grinzing Cemetry, to be followed, five years later, by Thomas Bernhard.

Acknowledgments

Unless otherwise mentioned, the photos are from the photo archive of the
Thomas Bernhard Nachlaßverwaltung GmbH (photos from the family's private
collection: mostly by Emil Fabjan, Rudolf Freumbichler, and Peter Fabjan)

Cover photo: Thomas Bernhard in Sintra 1987   Peter Fabjan

Additional photos were provided by:

Hilde Zuckerstätter	p. 37 top left
Christian Strasser	p. 43
Rudolf Neuböck	p. 59 bottom right
Ingrid Bülau	p. 91
Gerda Maleta	p. 130
Liselotte von Uexküll	p. 146
Kurt Osinger	p. 164, 174, 175, 176, 177
Rudolf Brändle	p. 171, 186 middle, 187, 202
Ferry Radax	p. 195

Quotations from Bernhard's texts were taken from the following translations:

Gathering Evidence. A Memoir
(A Child, An Indication of the Cause,
The Cellar, Breath, In the Cold) in this book, p. 8 (trans. David McLintock, New York: Vintage 1993, p. 125), p. 24 (p. 21), p. 25
(pp. 20f.), p. 34 (p. 21), p. 37 (p. 308), p. 38 (pp. 128f.), p. 40 (pp. 30f.), p. 41 (p. 20), p. 43 (pp. 43-46),
p. 44 (p. 44), p. 48 (p. 32), p. 50 (p. 35), p. 52 (pp. 183f.), p. 56 (p. 98), p. 59 (p. 100), p. 60 (p. 255).,
p. 185 (p. 337), p. 186 (p. 297)

Correction in this book, p. 24 (trans. Sophie Wilkens, New York: Knopf 1979, pp. 245f.)
Extinction in this book, p. 66 (trans. David McLintock, New York: Knopf 1995, p. 13, 143)
Heldenplatz in this book, p. 175 (trans. Gitta Honegger, in: *Conjunctions 33: Crossing Over. The Millenium Issue*,
New York: Bard College 1999, pp. 310, 312, 336)
Old Masters in this book, p. 203 (trans. Ewald Osers. London, New York: Quartet 1989, p. 143)
Ritter, Dene, Voss in this book, p. 176 (in: Histrionics. Three Plays. Trans. Peter Jansen and Kenneth Northcott. Chicago and
London: The University of Chicago Press 1990, p. 96).
Wittgenstein's Nephew in this book, p. 200 (trans. Ewald Osers, London: Quartet 1986, p. 19)

In all other cases the German versions of Bernhard's texts were translated:

Die Berühmten in this book, p. 8 (*Stücke 2*, Frankfurt am Main: Suhrkamp 1988, p. 173)
Elisabeth II in this book, p. 202 (*Stücke 4*, Frankfurt am Main: Suhrkamp 1988, p. 355)
Gesammelte Gedichte in this book, p. 23 (Frankfurt am Main: Suhrkamp 1991, p. 15)

Further texts that were also translated:

Rudolf Brändle (*Zeugenfreundschaft*) in this book, p. 177 (Salzburg, Vienna: Residenz 1999, p. 120f.),
p. 182 (p. 65ff.), p. 185 (p. 64f.), p. 187 (p. 59f.)

Ferry Radax (in: Maria Fialik: *Der Charismatiker. Thomas*
Bernhard und die Freunde von einst) in this book, p. 195 (Vienna: Böhlau 1992, p. 170)
Asta Scheib (in: *Von einer Katastrophe in die andere. 13 Ge-*
spräche mit Thomas Bernhard. Ed. by Sepp Dreissinger) in this book, p. 160 (Weitra: Bibliothek der Provinz 1992,
p. 137), p. 179 (p. 141), p. 191 (p.. 141), p. 201 (p. 140)